Beliefology

Raise Your Consciousness to Wealth, Health and Happiness!!!

❧ ❧ ❧ ❧

Kenneth Routson

TuliP
Press
Fairfield, Ohio

Cover Artwork by: AmeriPress
Layout and Design by: Denise J. Lasley
Printed by: Bookmasters, Inc.
Published by: Tulip Press
        P.O. Box 181212
        Fairfield, OH 45018

Material based on *BELIEFOLOGY* © 1997

First Edition   10 9 8 7 6 5 4 3 2 1

Library of Congress Catalog Card Number: 97-61108
International Standard Book Number (ISBN): 978-1-891067-05-1

ACKNOWLEDGMENTS

My first acknowledgment of thanks is to Denise Lasley for her editing and general support in assisting me in bringing **BELIEFOLOGY** to fruition and to Del Lasley for his narration of **BELIEFOLOGY** for audio reproduction.

And I am eternally grateful to my students throughout the country, as well as my friends and teachers who all encouraged me to write this book. The experiences they have shared with me over the years have contributed significantly to the concepts expressed in this book.

DEDICATION

I dedicate this book to my partner in life, Leslie Stewart, who's shared journey and numerous hours of discussion and dreaming led to many of the ideas and experiences in ***BELIEFOLOGY***.

In loving appreciation to my mother, Fern Routson, for teaching me that there is strength in gentleness and the wisdom to believe in things unseen; my father, Kenneth Routson, for teaching me unconditional love; Karl and Martha Stewart, Gordon Stonehouse, my brothers, sisters, Paula and my other nieces and nephews.

TABLE OF CONTENTS

FOREWORD
❧ ❦ ❧ ❦

Ken Routson and I first met 25 years ago in one of life's delightful synchronicities.

I had noticed that the song *"Is That All There Is?"* was a constant intruder in my consciousness. Something was obviously missing in my externally-focused life. There was a vague angst, but nothing specific.

Then a friend suggested the *SETH* material by Jane Roberts, where the underlying theme is, "You create your own reality." It resonated deeply in suggesting ways to reclaim one's personal power through inner-direction. I craved dialogue with like-minded people. And one day in the personal classified ads of the daily paper -- a section I rarely read -- was an ad for a *SETH* Seminar. BINGO!! The workshop was being conducted by Ken at the Fontainbleau Hotel in Miami Beach, right down the street from my home! I was off and running on my journey of awakening.

A few years later, my hundreds of little scraps of daily-transcribed thoughts emerged from their shoebox and became the personal journal that is *THE GURU IS YOU*.

Subsequently, there were additional learning experiences and more published books. Ken and I would talk from time to time about how the game of life seemed such an interesting paradox. *Wasn't it perfect, either for our enjoyment or our growth? Weren't we constantly jolted out of our lethargy and given new wake-up calls by dynamic situations that provided exactly what was needed for our maximum growth?* Life can be such a humbling experience.

Ken's *BELIEFOLOGY* concept is right on the money. Our belief systems do indeed attract corresponding life events. Positive or negative experiences are causally created by underlying thoughts, ideas and beliefs. Thus the need to re-focus inward, identify limiting beliefs, and do the necessary work to help ourselves.

This book fills an important need in today's overwritten market of pop psychology and metaphysical esoterica. It is practical, well written, and valuable to all levels of readership in helping to take charge of one's life.

Congratulations, Ken. We've come a long way, haven't we, friend?

Martin Segal
President, New Age Publishing Co.

And the author of:

THE GURU IS YOU, How To Play and Win the Game of Life

PEELING THE SWEET ONION, Unlayering the Veils of Identity and Existence

BLAME IT ON THE BUDDHISTS, and Other Stories

INTRODUCTION

৶ ৸ ৶ ৸

Ten years ago in the introduction of the first edition of BELIEFOLOGY, I wrote that I wanted to introduce the grass roots community to "the best kept secret of the ages": you create 100% of your personal reality and co-create your collective reality. Since then, I have appreciated the many letters and calls from individuals all over the world who have told me that BELIEFOLOGY has completely transformed their lives.

Recently others have captivated the world on major international television broadcasts with their own secret regarding the Law of Attraction. Many people who have either attended my Beliefology workshops or come to me for life coaching have expressed to me that the critics of these broadcasts don't really understand the bigger picture of the law of attraction. They have expressed their feeling that BELIEFOLOGY is more comprehensive than the incomplete, simplistic version of this universal law being touted. It's their perception that BELIEFOLOGY provides a broader perspective; a true picture of how co-operation, authentic power, health, joy and prosperity are really our true nature and how it is our belief in lack, limitation, judgment, guilt, undeservability, evil, separateness from God and feelings of unworthiness that prevent us from having our life of choice. What BELIEFOLOGY does have in common with these new products is a *belief* that anyone can be, do or have anything they want!

Finally I knew that the secret was out and that I needed to reprint BELIEFOLOGY. My editor and I agreed that it would be a long time before BELIEFOLOGY could ever become outdated because as my inspirational teacher once told me

"Beliefology is a concept whose time has come, has always been, and will always be."

The concepts in this book are not original. You'll find them in literature, films and plays. Knowledgeable people such as Einstein, Khalil Gibran, William James, Emerson, Budda, Louise Hay and others also embraced much of this knowing. The essence of this philosophy is that your beliefs -- defined as "something that is trusted or believed" -- combined with emotions, intent and expectations, affect your consciousness and create your life.

Consciousness is the root, the source, the cause, or you might say the "stuff" that is everything and everybody. We literally create our lives from the smallest event to the most significant happening. Our conscious thoughts, beliefs, ideas, and emotions are transmitted into energy frequencies that act as magnets that attract events. Therefore, if we emotionally think and believe constructive, positive, non-limiting thoughts, the corresponding consciousness will draw in favorable life experiences. Conversely, fearful, limiting, negative thinking and beliefs will result in undesirable events. More and more people throughout the world are realizing the universal truth that when you transform your consciousness you can have the life you truly desire.

It is advantageous to evaluate your beliefs in order to discover why you attract the people and the events in your life. Since many people have accepted most of their erroneous beliefs about themselves and the world from "authorities" outside of themselves, it may be beneficial to question your current assumptions and explore your current beliefs. So I've come up with this book, *BELIEFOLOGY,* that is a *DO-IT-YOURSELF* study of beliefs and how they co-create the world.

The purpose of *BELIEFOLOGY* is to help you identify your beliefs and how they impact your life, as well as the study of *SELF* and the exploration of Self and its relationship with God and the universe.

I encourage each and every reader to be skeptical about the contents of this book. My only request is that you consider the possibilities. Most of the problems in our personal lives, as well as the problems of society at large, are because we blindly accept beliefs about ourselves, God and the universe that are simply limiting, detrimental and often harmful. Observe the beliefs of your family, friends and co-workers and determine for yourself if their thoughts, beliefs and emotions create their fortunes or misfortunes, their health or illness, their abundance or lack, their happiness or unhappiness.

Many people will initially agree with the concept that we create our own lives, until they realize that I'm saying that this means literally every event -- there are no accidents, no victims and no coincidences! In other words, if you're involved in an accident, robbery, rape, natural disaster or domestic abuse, you're not a victim, because on some level of consciousness you attracted that experience according to your belief system. Yes, I am saying that even in a fatal plane crash, every person (usually unconsciously) acquiesces to the event, while others will change their future by drawing in a "co-incidence" that will cause the potential "victim" to miss the flight.

Currently "victimhood" is socially acceptable and many people would wonder about my sanity for believing that it's the victim's beliefs that attract the events. Nevertheless, I'm one of many that are taking complete responsibility for consciously creating my reality of choice. I have made significant progress, especially in the areas of abundance, career and relationships. You can too. But even as you make progress, you will discover you have *so much more* potential to grow. You will gain success in some life areas faster than others. It's critical not to compare your situation with others, because the time it takes to manifest your preferred results is relative. It's been my personal experience, as well as the observations of my students, that belief work regarding the physical body often takes longer to manifest because it requires a transformation of cellular consciousness. It may take longer for some people to change their consciousness than others because they may have more erroneous beliefs to unlearn or many more years of emotional habitual patterns to retrain.

There were two personal reasons that motivated me to write this book. The primary purpose is to help others improve their lives. In retrospect, I'm often amazed at the progress I've made in my life. Once I was an insecure, fearful person, with an incredible inferiority complex. I know if *I* can change my belief systems and consequently transform my life into a much more fulfilled, happy, joyful and prosperous reality, then I know its possible for anyone to do it. Although I offer seminars and individual classes to teach the philosophies and techniques that have been successful to me, many have encouraged me to write a book that they could lend to a friend in need.

My other personal reason is to help others so they will not have to suffer needlessly as my father and sister did. My father lost his leg when he was young because of diabetes, suffered a paralyzing stroke and died soon after his 57th birthday. My sister prostituted herself to support her twenty-year heroine addiction and died at 45 years "young" from sclerosis of the liver. She was HIV positive when she died. Most people don't enjoy suffering, whether because of illness, financial poverty, unhappiness or loneliness. I know my father and sister didn't. Conditions were what they were in their lives because of ignorance. Hopefully, this book can help others help themselves.

Finally, along with techniques to raise your consciousness to wealth, health and happiness, we will examine historical and existing paradigms that are the basis for our current systems and institutions. Education, child rearing, the judicial system, corporations, organized religion, science and medicine have much of their framework centered around limiting, outdated, collective beliefs -- based on the paternal, authoritarian, hierarchical mentality. For the next ten years, human beings, mother earth and all its creatures will witness a spiritual awakening and the most drastic transformation in consciousness ever experienced on this planet. This new awareness will stir each individual to new epiphanies so that individuals can reclaim their power and declare freedom from the outer control of these institutions that no longer serve their purpose. The aforementioned social systems are in the beginning stages of crumbling themselves out of existence. Consequently, the entire planet is evolving and will impact every person, animal, plant, organization, community and nation as well as the climate and geography, and will culminate in trillions of new opportunities.

I will explain how concepts, such as judgment with all of its implications, have influenced the foundation of our society and how they affect so many of our personal and mass beliefs.

Lastly and most important, we will discuss the major ingredients of **BELIEFOLOGY** -- trust and unconditional love. You can have all sorts of beneficial mental beliefs, but if you don't trust and believe in yourself and accept that the universe is good, abundant and is always for you, then all the positive mental beliefs are futile. Living happy, joyful and fulfilled in the moment while loving yourself, others and the world unconditionally is the ultimate goal of **BELIEFOLOGY**.

1 THE POWER OF THE MIND

Thought

Most of my life I have studied, through observation and experience, the power of the mind and how we all create our life through our beliefs. Many may refute me by saying, "Well, it's not scientific." That's true. It is my opinion that science and medicine could be even further along today if both disciplines would be willing to go beyond the physical. So many of the physicians, psychologist, and scientists who have attended my classes have said to me, "Ken, if I can't see it, or feel it than it doesn't exist!" I always respond, "You can't see the wind, gravity, or electricity either. Nevertheless, we are affected by their existence constantly."

It is unbelievable how advanced humans have become in the area of modern technology and it has been predicted that with the new sophisticated computers, as well as fiber/cyber technology, our world will be transformed more in the next 10 years than in the entire history of our known civilization. Conversely, with all the advancements in the aforementioned technologies, socially and emotionally we seem to be further away from optimal health, fulfillment and happiness.

Much to my amazement, people continue to place too much confidence, belief and security in things outside themselves, while still feeling so powerless and insecure in regard to their ability to be in charge of their own lives. Clearly it is believed possible to push a button on a garage door opener to raise the garage door, but what a novel idea (not to mention frightening) when in my seminars I explain how your thoughts attract events. The skeptics begin to revolt.

You may think the mind functions much like that automatic door opener, computers, television and radio. But in reality the opposite is true. All inventions are reflections of how we create our personal reality. Just as it is stated in Genesis that God created man in his image, accordingly man -- and women -- make most of their creations in their own image.

It is assumed that the brain is the home of our mind and therefore the control tower. Recently there has been a revolution in that thinking that defines the mind as a form of consciousness, or you could even say spirit. And this spirit/consciousness actually exists before the brain and after -- meaning before birth and after death.

The brain is the physical agent that acts as the biocomputer, and the mind is the operator. My favorite quote in reference to this phenomenon is one from Wayne Dyer: "You are not a physical being having a spiritual experience, but a spiritual being having a physical experience." With the advent of the mind-body connection, the future of medicine will be transformed in unbelievable ways. We will be required to assume responsibility for our health. We will be unable to fall victim to germs, genetics, and allergies and, instead of relying on medicine, we will learn to take charge of our lives by changing our beliefs and living from a point of power. We will talk more about "point of power" later in the book.

The most important characteristic of the mind is *thoughts*. I teach that thoughts are energy and energy is power. Most of what I will be discussing in this book is not new but universal laws and principles that have been expressed by metaphysicians and progressive psychic and spiritual teachers throughout the years. Eastern philosophies and religions probably come closer to certain universal truths than western thinking. But many of these ideas have been distorted over time or are presented as only half-truths.

For instance many people influenced by eastern thinking believe that the physical world and our bodies are just an illusion. They limit themselves in interpreting Eastern philosophy on non-attachment by declaring that desire, whether sexual or for material gain, is negative and anti-spiritual. Conversely, I believe that the universe is full of material abundance and it is our natural inheritance to accept material prosperity. Only when we repress, suppress or depress our natural desires do we create disease, emotionally as well as physically.

THE PREREQUISITE OF CREATIVITY IS DESIRE.

I agree with the organizations of Eastern thought that non-attachment is healthier than clinging to possessions and relationships. I will expand further on this subject later in the book. But it is my opinion that instead of denying the physical world, including our bodies, we should understand that our thought process is an effect that is interconnected within and governed by a much larger, self-knowing, conscious, omnipotent, creatively expressive, super intelligent consciousness. In other words, thought is a "not yet" physical idea that is composed of electromagnetic units of awareized energy. And the intensity of the thought via the "e-motion" will determine the speed and results of the consequential physical manifestation.

The Power of the Mind:
Beliefs

For many of you, the following concepts may seem foreign. And some of you may intellectually accept these universal laws, however you may have difficulty actually transforming former beliefs into constructive beliefs and consequently into new, desired events. Once you begin to realize that your beliefs create your life and, more important, can indeed create prosperity, good health and harmonious relationships, you will be a teacher for many people in your life even if it is only through example.

Beliefs are thoughts that are organized into ideas about self, others, God or the universe. You could say they are assumptions that are usually regarded as *FACTS about LIFE!* Most of these so-called "FACTS" are only "BELIEFS" or attitudes we have accepted as "TRUTHS" from our parents, churches, school and life in general.

YOU CREATE YOUR REALITY THROUGH YOUR BELIEFS, THOUGHTS, EMOTIONS AND INTENT!

Therefore it is your beliefs that dictate all of the circumstances in your life, including the people you meet, events and the physical objects you will own, as well as your health. This concept is not a new one, but it has transformed my life and the lives of many of my students. When you truly accept this awareness, you can take charge of your life and become the master magician of your thinking and beliefs, choosing only those beliefs that will attract the best to your life.

We are entering an exciting, exhilarating, revolutionary time when more and more human beings are transforming the overall consciousness with the realization of this phenomenon.

Collectively we have been conditioned to believe that circumstances *happen to us* and that conditions are *forced upon us*. That is just not true. We are actually the author of our life's play, and the actor, choreographer and the audience. To continue with this analogy, life is a play and we cast *every character* from the most significant relationship (wife, husband, children) to the most casual person (clerk, pedestrian, waitress/waiter) we encounter on life's stage. I will illustrate in a subsequent chapter just how your inner self translates your intent and expectations into physical manifestations.

Beliefs have even stronger electromagnetic realities than just mere fragmented thoughts.

LIKE ATTRACTS LIKE!

Similar beliefs will gather among themselves, organizing ideas or attitudes that create emotions that further enhance conviction. The purpose of this book, **BELIEFOLOGY,** is to assist you in your study about beliefs, their origins and consequences. Essentially **BELIEFOLOGY** is based on three primary beliefs: the assumptions we have about God, the world and ourselves. In essence, we are simultaneously all three of these realities. However, for examination and communication purposes we will study them individually.

From these primary beliefs -- our self-image, our perception of God (or spiritual beliefs) and how we perceive the world -- we form tributary root ideas or beliefs that create our everyday life and its experiences.

PRIMARY BELIEFS	**ROOT BELIEFS**
A. Spiritual Beliefs	1. Health & Vitality
	2. Money/Resources: Material Things
B. Self image (perception)	3. Personality Character / Self Esteem
	4. Relationship
	5. Work/Career
C. Belief about world	6. Religious/Spiritual

Later you will see how these beliefs are interconnected and the effect they have on your conscious reality.

The Power of the Mind:
You Are What You Think

Now it is time for you to become a beliefologist and explore your beliefs to be able to recognize any erroneous beliefs, or false perceptions of reality or fact that you may have about either yourself or the world.

As you examine your personal belief profile, you will discover many hidden beliefs you may have accepted blindly -- beliefs you have learned from parents, teachers, religion, siblings, friends, your community, your country and the world.

As children we need our parents and society to provide us with organization, structure and basic tools to operate effectively. However, I believe that most of the disease, poverty, crime, hatred, bigotry, war, dysfunctional families and poor self-esteem in this world is because we simply accept much of what we were taught by those "Authorities." For many adults their self-talk and their responses to life, politics and religion -- essentially the way they act or don't act -- have much to do with the "truths" they claimed as children.

In addition we have collective and cultural beliefs. Let's take a look at the major evolution of some of these mass beliefs. For instance, remember when humans believed the world was flat, or a time, not that long ago, when people believed man could never fly, much less walk on the moon?

And what about the changes in attitude about the foods we eat? When I was in school, meat (even red meat) and milk were a recommended part of the diet. But gradually the very part of the diet that was supposed to be the "good" became the "bad" food. The "evils" of certain foods were sold to us collectively from the "authorities": the medical and scientific committees. Hence the fear campaign had begun. We were bombarded from every form of media: "Look out for the sugar monster, it will make your kids hyperactive." "Beware of salt, it can cause high blood pressure!" Who had ever heard of cholesterol until the eighties? The labs loved it -- more tests -- *MORE MONEY*! Yes, fear sells!

Oh, and let's not forget the current fad -- FAT!! It's amazing that even after all the public service announcements, medical studies/lectures and the billions of dollars in commercials to sell these scare tactics, there are more hyperactive and fat kids now then there were before when it was socially acceptable for grandma to spoil their grandchildren with lots of sugar whether it was cookies, pies, fried chicken, steaks or roast beef.

Unless you have a serious health condition, I don't think any of the aforementioned evil food culprits are bad for your health *if you enjoy them in moderation.* In fact, the guilt, anger and frustration we experience when we focus on our inability to control the urge to overdo when we indulge in these foods are far more damaging then the food itself. Yes, I think balance is the key! Contrary to the belief "You are what you eat", I subscribe more to the belief "You are what you think!" Even though I think diet is important -- especially amounts, the time we eat and why -- I believe it's more important to examine what we put into our minds. If we spent even 10% of the time and energy we place in thinking about what we put in our mouths into thinking about what we put into our heads, we would be healthier, wealthier and, most important, happier!

The Power of the Mind:
From Belief To Manifestation

Unlike many psychologists, psychiatrists, hypno-therapists and other schools of thought, I believe we create our life from our conscious mind and I don't think it's necessary to dive into the deep sub-conscious to find the origins of a problem. I think the answer to the cause of a problem can be found right here, right now, in your conscious mind. You may *choose* to make it unconscious by not taking the time to become aware of your self-talk or to determine your conscious thoughts to find out what it is you really believe and not just what you say you believe.

In fact, you may *choose* to ignore or even fear to observe unconscious beliefs because they are "bad", limiting, embarrassing or harmful. But it can be your *choice* to see, observe, and bring to consciousness those unconscious beliefs. Later you will learn not only how to change those limiting beliefs but how to reclaim your inherent power to replace them with empowering ones.

BELIEFS CREATE OUR REALITY!

It's your conscious mind that sends your intent -- which contains your conscious beliefs -- to your inner self. And your inner self is connected to your oversoul, which is connected to the God-self that makes everything -- visible to invisible -- possible. This process is electromagnetic in nature and its ability to organize, create and communicate would make our most sophisticated computers look simple! And your inner self will only bring to your outer life those experiences, events and circumstances your conscious mind agrees with and believes possible.

9

One of the most important functions of the conscious mind is to evaluate physical experience and discriminate between which events we choose to continue and which experiences we choose to change. Often we reinforce our erroneous beliefs by rationalizing our experiences. If you see your marriage end in a bitter divorce, more numbers in your black book are doctors and attorneys than friends and you struggle to pay your bills and maybe end up unemployed, then chances are you may say, "Ken, I've got the proof that my life is terrible!" But things will materialize according to your conscious mind, even though many times your inner-self, via intuition, suggests that your conscious mind make a different choice.

Conversely, if you're the epitome of abundant health, your relationships are plentiful and harmonious, you are thriving financially and, most important, you're happy and at peace with yourself, you have some very constructive and beneficial conscious beliefs.

Earlier we broke down our primary beliefs into six major root beliefs: Health & Vitality; Money & Resources (material things); Personality Character/Self Esteem; Relationships; Work/Career; and Religious/Spiritual. The following are only a sample of erroneous beliefs in each of these categories. How may of these may be limiting your life?

Health & Vitality
1.   Life is a bitch.
2.   Dress warm or you will catch a cold.
3.   I am weak because I was a sickly child.
4.   Don't drink from someone's glass; you'll catch their germs.
5.   I inherited it because it's in my genes.
6.   I'm too old for that.
7.   I'm being punished for another lifetime.
8.   I'm a bad person.
9.   Jesus suffered for our sins.

10. No pain - No gain!
11. What's the use?
12. Beware of viruses.

Money Resources / Material Things
1. Money is the root of all evil.
2. She's poor as a church mouse.
3. There's not enough to go around.
4. People with money are greedy.
5. Power corrupts.
6. You have to step on others to make it big.
7. You can't be rich and spiritual.
8. I always have bad luck.
9. There's not enough money.
10. I have no imagination and I'm definitely not creative.
11. People who drive luxury cars are snobs.
12. If I had a degree, I could earn more money.

Personality / Character / Self Esteem
1. I must be punished for what I did.
2. I must work harder to overcome my laziness.
3. I must lose weight in order to love myself.
4. The world is in trouble because we need more laws.
5. If you're good, you'll be rewarded and if you're bad, you'll be punished.
6. I'll be successful and acceptable when I lose weight and can afford fashionable clothing.
7. God is a vengeful god, primarily masculine, who judges his creations.
8. I have always been weak, without any will power.
9. I have no control over what happens to me.
10. I am too weak.
11. I am unworthy; I have no right to happiness.
12. It's too good to be true; now what's going to happen?

Relationships
1. Once I lose weight I'll attract my prince charming.
2. Men are all after the same thing.
3. You can't trust anyone now days.
4. Women are only after your money.
5. I abuse children because I was abused as a child.
6. She stuck with him until death. There's a place in heaven for her.
7. Sexual thoughts are bad.
8. I think the father (or husband) should be the boss.
9. I'm too old to get married.
10. I can't be free in a relationship.
11. You can't have sex unless you're married.
12. He's jealous/possessive because he loves me.

Work / Career
1. Life is a struggle.
2. The more money I make, the more I spend.
3. You have to work hard to succeed.
4. Work isn't supposed to be fun.
5. I better stay where I am because I may not find another job.
6. I don't have any skills or abilities.
7. It's tough out there.
8. I don't have enough education.
9. I'm not worthy.
10. Male bosses are always stricter.
11. I'm afraid of responsibilities.
12. 9-5 jobs offer no creativity.

Religious/Spiritual

1. God is an all-knowing, powerful man.
2. We must worship God.
3. God rewards and punishes all people.
4. Suffering and/or hard work will guarantee you a place in heaven.
5. Heaven is a place where you go if you are good and hell is a place you will go if you are bad.
6. Money is the root of all evil and God looks fondly upon the poor.
7. Sex is bad.
8. Men are more important and powerful than women and should dominate in family, church and business.
9. Man is born with original sin and must be baptized and/or saved in order to enter heaven.
10. I am separate from God and nature.
11. I must protect myself and my family against the unsafe world.
12. I'm afraid because there is so much evil in the world.

2 | THE NATURE OF CONSCIOUSNESS

Consciousness is *"ALL THAT IS"*

Everything that exists, both physical and non-physical, is made up of units of consciousness. Trees, people, dirt, rocks, animals, as well as daydreams and night dreams are all different types of consciousness.

I'm not sure if anyone can actually define consciousness, it is so multi-dimensional. But in order to try to understand the many different types of consciousness, their roles and how they interact, lets start with some of the smallest ones.

Let's start with the human body and consider the millions of atoms and molecules that come together to become a cell. The sub-particles of these atoms and molecules are individual, awareized energy consciousness that vibrate faster than the atoms and molecules in our physical system until they merge into the electromagnetic properties of our physical universe. Of course, this is a general and simplified explanation, though it gives you enough of a picture to understand that the body is a Consciousness Gestalt that consists of many interdependent consciousnesses.

After the cells are formed, they unite to become body organs. In other words, some cell consciousnesses will choose to become a heart, some a kidney, while others will join together to become a part of the liver. Although all of the organs have their own consciousness, they cannot survive alone.

15

So the inner-self creates an invisible form that translates into a flesh structure. This process of spirit made flesh consists of invisible light and inaudible sound that subsequently becomes the body structure that we perceive. In essence, our physical form is actually pulsating light and sound -- all energy.

CONSCIOUSNESS SUPPLIES THE BLUEPRINT THAT DEFINES THE PHYSICAL FORM.

And all of the organs of the body have a neurological connection with the master control tower -- the human mind!

The mind also has its foundation in consciousness, because our consciousness is the culmination of our experiences, actions, ideas, thoughts, feelings, attitudes and beliefs.

And the mind has its roots in a much larger dimension that is also invisible but nevertheless significantly more powerful and creative -- the infinite cosmic consciousness. This cosmic consciousness is the higher universal intelligence that is the source of everything that is physical. Some refer to this energy essence as God. Others, including myself, choose to call it **ALL THAT IS!** This concept is so difficult to describe in words, I suggest you try to feel it instead of thinking it. Many of you may be visualizing a place. But it's not a place, like heaven, as much as an infinite process of inexhaustible energy, action, creativity and ever-exploding fulfillment. This everlasting process includes all of its creations, offspring and offshoots who are separate but of the same; unique but related; always individualized but paradoxically always a part of the whole; one of the same; ALL THAT IS; GOD; universal intelligence; or what ever you want to attempt to name it.

Don't let the word *"intelligence"* mislead you. This universal force that gives all of its parts is, in essence, awareized, unconditional love that expresses itself with feeling tones. In fact this expression is manifested in every fiber of existence, both physical and non-physical.

ALL THAT IS is like one, big ***Cosmic ORGASM!***

✢ ✢ ✢ ✢

Although different and unique, every natural substance on earth from animals, plants, trees, rocks, mountains, dirt and insects to humans is a product of consciousness. All that we experience is the product of consciousness. And all that we can imagine, consciousness can create. It is important to understand the concept of consciousness, but it is difficult to define something that is so extremely complex. Even God would have difficulty finding words in English to define consciousness. But we do know this -- consciousness is an all-encompassing, powerful and positive creative life force.

The Nature of Consciousness:
Your Perception of God

Much of your consciousness is determined by your belief, perception and image of God. For instance, if you believe in a jealous, fearful and judgmental God, then consequently you will most likely be jealous, manipulative in your relationships, controlling, suspicious and fearful in your personal and your business interactions. Furthermore, your actions, as well as your responses to life's events, will be deeply rooted in the framework of reward and punishment. If you believe in a judgmental God, you will most likely be outer-directed, meaning you will require someone else's validation, approval and permission to be happy. You will probably be extremely motivated to do "good", or do the right thing, because you believe there will be an external punishment if you don't!

This is what I believe: The God/Goddess is all that is...all that ever was and will be; an infinite, inexhaustible, all powerful, universal, ever creating Spirit, that expresses itself as a gestalt of consciousness and has the free will and freedom to individualize itself interdependently and cooperatively. Most important, its primary essence is an awareized, conscious, collective consciousness of unconditional love; continuously and simultaneously receiving/projecting fulfillment through its creations as it becomes more by allowing replications in the form of offshoots.

It is my belief that those who subscribe, and even more important, identify with this God, will exemplify this powerful, joyful, happy, unconditionally loving deity with a life of health, wealth, compassion and happiness. These people will enjoy harmonious relationships, will be inner-directed, will desire inner-fulfillment and will *understand* others who are suffering through their actions of ignorance instead of judging them.

Instead of promoting punishment, these individuals will encourage rehabilitation, enlightenment, self-love and acceptance and personal responsibility. If you subscribe to the beliefs that you create your reality and that you live, move and have your being in this collective *God-Hood*, then in addition you will also recognize that there can't be anything outside of this ALL THAT IS essence and that any so-called devils or Hell (in which I do not believe) or so-called victims of crime, disease or poverty are of the same God-Hood but are being expressed in unnatural ways, temporarily and artificially separating themselves from the God-Hood.

I often refer to myself as highly spiritual, but not religious and that usually confuses most people. I believe that most organized religions are based on dogma that has much of its origin in a controlled male-chauvinistic arena. In other words, the founders and subsequent believers identified with a controlling, male, manipulative being who must have been pretty insecure and inferior to have demanded his subordinates to worship and adore him or he would be quick to judge and possibly punish by hell, damnation or whatever he felt fitting. With this in mind, it is easy to understand how our current good-bad, right-wrong framework came about, including our justice (or if you will, our "injustice") system, correctional institutions, educational systems, child rearing practices and on and on.

As a child I read religious literature and listened to people engaged in religious conversation and I perceived God as a White Cosmic Santa Claus who interacted in people's affairs like a chess game, rewarding the weak, fearful, sick, subservient souls who pleaded forgiveness and took note of those naughty or wealthy souls who refused to repent. I would ask in Sunday school, "Are you telling me that those kids in Africa who are not exposed to Christianity and are therefore not baptized are sentenced to hell after this life?" Unfortunately, the answer was "Yes -- only through Jesus can you enter the kingdom of heaven." Even as a young child this didn't feel right to me.

Further study about this fearful, angry, insecure, deity left me feeling that if there is such a being that I refused to be subject to his wrath! Gradually I discovered within myself the God I now believe in. Because of this belief I eventually attracted others who perceived God as gentle but powerful, loving, a being that accepts all of his/her creations and grants freedom and permission to all of his/her children/creations to create their life of choice, even when it meant disease, hate and chaos.

Although we can never separate ourselves from God and All That Is can never be extracted from ourselves, we *can* feel separate and *choose*, consciously or by conditioning, to identify with unnatural characteristics like hate, scarcity, greed, judgment, guilt or sadness. God is freedom and allows freedom because it is so powerful it has *no-thing* to fear. This God consciousness therefore knows no boundaries and is forever becoming, fulfilling, expressing and exploring itself while simultaneously becoming more by procreating, and spawning even new universes. And each creation has its own identity and uniqueness but paradoxically is a part of and interacting with all the other identity personalities. This God extends freedom to all of its creation to choose -- good or bad, health or sickness, wealth or poverty, adversity or harmony, happiness or sadness. I believe that you make the choice!

3 | THE TRANSFORMATION OF YOUR CONSCIOUSNESS

Belief Awareness

In order for you to transform your consciousness it is imperative that you change your beliefs, raise your awareness, and break down your self-imposed boundaries. These measures will enhance your vibrations and attract new people, events and experiences that correspond to your new consciousness. But for the most part it is difficult to change a belief if you're not sure what your beliefs are.

The best way to identify your belief is to objectively observe each area of your life. It's extremely important to observe your self-talk because not only will this help you learn about your beliefs, but your self-talk is the major catalyst for changing your old beliefs. Self-talk is merely thoughts and thoughts develop into beliefs and whatever we believe to be true becomes reality as long as we believe it.

Then your beliefs form your emotions, so it is equally important to be in touch with your emotions. Essentially, most negative beliefs/attitudes are based on fear! We always get what we concentrate on, and boy, do we know that when it comes to fear. The anatomy of fear is a belief in basic powerlessness, lack of trust and a belief that life is a struggle and that life doesn't support us. In the area of abundance, fear is created from the belief that there is only so much energy, resources, food, money, etc. to go around, instead of believing in an unlimited source of abundance that is the true nature of the universe.

In addition to listening to your self-talk and observing your emotions, it's also beneficial to be aware of your habitual responses to life's experiences. If you're still dubious and skeptical about this idea of creating your reality through your beliefs, then instead of observing your own life, pay attention to your fellow workers, family members or a friend's life. Are certain people more accident-prone? Are some chronic complainers? Do any have never ending stories about how another boss screwed them again?

Conversely, you may know others who turn everything they touch to gold, attract friends and opportunities easily and effortlessly and have impeccable health and vitality. You may even know some centenarians that are in better mental and physical shape then many people in their fifties. Examine their beliefs and I'm sure you will discover the reason! It's often easier to see other people's beliefs than your own. We have a tendency to put on defensive blinders and often either ignore certain beliefs or rationalize others. Because of this, I was able to uncover some of my erroneous beliefs while I assisted others in identifying their beliefs.

Once you have discovered your erroneous beliefs, it's time to change them. Sometimes it only takes the awareness and the realization of an erroneous belief and then like magic your consciousness is transformed without the formal exercises of affirmations and visualizations. Many of the books, tapes and teachers (especially in the early days) that I'm familiar with suggest that you set up a specific time to do affirmations and visualizations. Yes, I believe structured exercises may be beneficial, however, I recommend you integrate affirmations and visualization into the natural process of everyday living.

An affirmation is defined as a statement that is written and or spoken in the present tense that <u>affirms</u> what it is you want to manifest in your life. It is always recommended to be as specific and positive as possible. There is power in repetition and it is common practice to say and write affirmations over and over with much conviction.   Remember, you get what you concentrate on!   But this method can backfire and you may unknowingly be reinforcing your negative beliefs. Even though you are affirming out loud "I am prosperous", on the inside your self-talk may be in conflict with thoughts like, "Yes, but I still don't know how I'm going to pay the rent next month," or "I don't have any skills." These thoughts negate any value from repeating the affirmations.

Visualization, often referred to as mental imagery, is a mental picture of anything you would like to manifest in your life. This can be anything from something material like a new car, house or job, to an intangible like happiness or peace with self and others. Your life is the result of all of your mental imagery, so these mental pictures precede reality and whatever your current image is, it will determine your next day, month or year unless your image changes.

I spent several years doing affirmations and visualization techniques everyday and didn't see much change in my life. However, when I started to examine my beliefs and change my erroneous beliefs and my overall attitude, as well as enhance my trust level of myself and life, then my life began to change! If you utilize affirmation/visualization in tandem with belief work, then you will be guaranteed results. For example, if you are visualizing healing a certain illness or body part, in reality what you're doing is concentrating on the problem instead of the solution -- health. In fact, it may be beneficial to ignore the disease and place more focus on visualization and imagining feeling great and seeing yourself doing something you enjoy. Although a structured exercise of affirmation and visualization may be beneficial, it is far more effective to *think* your affirmations and transfer this into your everyday life.

LIVE YOUR NEW POSITIVE AFFIRMATIONS!

When you visualize, make the image as clear and real as possible. In addition, it is necessary to use your emotions with enthusiasm and ZEST to *feel* the desired manifestations. As I stated earlier, the "e-motion" gives the idea or the mental image the fuel and the *motion* to become physical. Utilize imagination. It's one of our most valuable human resources! Imagine whatever it is you want in a way that is so real that you become what it is you want. That's the message of **BELIEFOLOGY**! *You have to identify and consciously be what you desire and only then will your life be that manifestation.* So if you're currently sick and tired you must *say* to yourself and then *vividly imagine* how you would wake up each morning feeling healthy, energetic and confident to pursue each and every task throughout that day with joy, happiness and vitality!

A friend of mine once asked another, "Have you been be-having yourself?" What he meant was not "Have you been being good" but "Have you been being like everything it is you wish to be (be-having)?" With this in mind, if you want a loving, kind relationship then *be* loving and kind to yourself and others. In order to draw in money and financial opportunities *be* generous and giving of yourself and your talents. If you want a new car, act and feel like your current car is a Mercedes. Or wear your current clothes as if they were those quality designer clothes of your dreams. BUT BEWARE!! Don't go out and put yourself in debt to buy these things right away because it may take a while to replace your old consciousness with your new consciousness. While you are doing your affirmations, whether it's during the day or during a structured exercise period, if you find your inner-talk and your beliefs are in conflict stop and work on changing the belief. It's only when you're aware of your self-doubts and fears that you can act to convert them to trust and active performance. You can read all the positive thinking books and listen to all the subliminal tapes in the world, but if you don't eradicate your erroneous beliefs and transform your consciousness then you will continue to get more of the same. As Einstein once said, "No problem can be solved from the same consciousness that created it."

So you can see, it is essential to think affirmatively, but you must be <u>consciously</u> <u>aware</u> of your response to everyday occurrences because they will be your feedback to what it is you really believe. It takes time from the moment we change a belief mentally for it to affect the emotional level and subsequently to transpire physically. Once the unconscious accepts those new beliefs given by the conscious mind and they are not in conflict, and all your actions concur, then your inner identity along with its electromagnetic patterning will undergo a restructuring. Consequently, these new frequencies will act as a powerful magnet and they will go out into the outer world and connect with people that have like inner frequencies of consciousness and you will "draw in" to your life new experiences. But it takes time, not only to re-pattern your consciousness, but also for all of your future life synchronicities to take place.

So act as if you were, and you will be. How you identify yourself and your world will predict and bring you possibilities or close your probabilities.

LIFE IS NOT LIMITING YOU -- YOU LIMIT YOURSELF.

Life is a smorgasbord of prosperity, happiness and fulfilling opportunities. You choose which experiences you will select from that universal smorgasbord!

4 CONSCIOUS LIFE CREATIONS

Earlier I broke down root beliefs into six major categories. Now let's look at some examples of **BELIEFOLOGY** and how your every day life is a reflection of your consciousness as it applies to these beliefs. The following examples are based on the lives of students I've assisted over the last seventeen years.

HEALTH & VITALITY

After attending one of my workshops on changing your beliefs, I was approached by a woman who asked for more help on how to transform her consciousness. The first assignment I gave her was to develop a *Personal Belief Profile*. I suggested that she prioritize the areas she wanted to improve, and decide which ones she wanted to start focusing on first. This woman felt she should try to improve her health because once she accomplished that, she would have more energy to devote to her career. The three major diseases in her body were recurring hemorrhoids, headaches and neck aches.

I reminded her of the concepts we discussed in the workshop regarding the mind-body connection -- how illness and injuries due to accidents are a reflection of something going on in our lives. Since she was unsure of what beliefs or what experiences in her life might be causing her physical symptoms, I suggested she become aware of where the pain seemed to be and when it seemed to increase. Finally, through conscious awareness and discernment, she determined that her neck hurt worse when she was driving home from work and her head ached worse on the weekends, but she wasn't sure about the hemorrhoids. Initially she thought the neck problems were the result of job stress, but she later discovered that the source of both the neck pain and the headache problems was her relationship with her husband.

This woman had been married to her husband for twenty years, and for most of that period her husband worked the second shift at his job. She realized that she had headaches on weekends through most of their marriage, and her neck aches as well as her hemorrhoids started after their children left the nest and her husband changed shifts so that in addition to the weekends he was now spending time with his wife in the evenings. So, readers, do you get it yet? Yes, this man was a *pain in his wife's ass!* He was a *pain in her neck!*

Earlier I discussed the importance of becoming aware of your self-talk. It's beneficial to *consciously* listen to the words that may be creating your reality. I made this woman aware of a conversation I overheard between her and workshop participants during a lunch break at my workshop. I must have heard her declare at least three times that this thing, person or place "was a pain in the ass!" Now I believe there are no victims. Not only did this woman choose to marry and stay with this man, she chose her emotional and physical response toward this person. We so often give our power away to others. This woman had the choice to end her relationship and to reclaim her power. Eventually this couple agreed that the only reason their marriage lasted as long as it did was because of the children. After their divorce, her aches and pains went away. Divorces can end in peaceful, cooperative partings. Instead of blaming others for your misfortunes, assume responsibility for your life and don't give up your power, especially the power of choice.

The two most feared diseases are cancer and AIDS. Students, relatives and friends I've known, whether they have overcome cancer or died, all seemed to be guilt ridden. The cancer, or what I believe to be the mental/emotional causation -- *Guilt* -- was literally eating them up! Their sense of desperate despair and powerlessness culminated in a "what's the use" attitude. Unfortunately there were a few individuals who claimed to be confident, hopeful and certain of a healing because of their belief in either Jesus or God. I believe their belief in either higher power wasn't enough to convince their "healthy cells" because they were unwilling to make the necessary changes in their lives. So often illness and accidents are merely warning signs from our physical vehicles informing the driver (our conscious mind) that we need to find or return to our life's purpose and make certain adjustments in our lives.

One man who requested my assistance, spent too much of his energy on being angry at the doctors for giving him a short time to live. Although I agreed with him that it would be difficult to do, I encouraged him to try to focus and direct his attention and, therefore, his energy on living, instead of the cancer and the anger. In addition I suggested that it was imperative that he work from a point of power and to attempt not to get sucked into the powerlessness. His typical response was, "I give up all my power to Christ Jesus and he will heal me from this dreadful disease."

I explained to this man that according to the philosophy to which I subscribe, God is like the power and light company. In order to be healed he would have to develop a partnership with God by plugging himself into the power outlet and turning on his light switch (conscious mind). The light switch is an analogy for our conscious mind and our ability to tap into -- or limit -- the flow and power of life. So often in times of peril or pending danger we "hope" that an outside force like God will save us. Nothing can save us from ourselves except our selves. Through our conscious mind and our beliefs we can provide energy to make what we want happen, or we can block that flow with doubt, fear and anxiety. Turn on the switch for light and life or turn off the power and let in "dis-ease" and darkness. Unfortunately, this man died after much pain and suffering.

I do not believe that anyone can heal another person without a sincere desire on the part of the person with the disease to get well. It doesn't matter how impressive the healer's credentials or reputation are, or whether he or she is a medical physician, psychic healer, faith healer, medicine man or an alternative practitioner. There must be a mutual collaboration between the patient and the healer and the patient must be receptive to the idea of getting well. I also believe that it is not necessary to have any assistance, because essentially all healing is self-healing, and the very nature of life, and the physical body has a natural propensity towards healing. Nevertheless, if a person with an illness truly believes in his/her practitioner or medicine, then such a belief can act as a catalyst to speed up or perhaps enhance the natural healing process.

During the early seventies, an oncologist began taking cancer patients that the AMA had given death sentences to, and helping them develop and use visualization and mental imagery techniques to make them well. This doctor had a very positive success rate with these previously diagnosed terminally ill patients. But I believe that those patients that didn't address the causes in their personal lives, could again "fall victim" to another disease or die in an accident if they didn't find their reason to live. In order to maintain good health after the healing, it is imperative that the cause of the illness or accident is resolved. Remember the cause is either an erroneous belief in an area of your life that's out of control, or the need to discover and follow your life's purpose.

Illness is the result of misdirected energy. There is no good energy or bad energy but just energy that can be utilized in a positive (favorable and natural) or negative (unfavorable, unnatural) manner. You often hear metaphysicians state, "Your life is the out-picturing of your consciousness" or "your body is spirit made flesh." Earlier in this book I mentioned that the events in your life are the products of your consciousness. Your body reflects your consciousness and is a biological barometer measuring the condition of your life and giving you a reading to help you make future decisions. So many of our diseases, aches, pains or general discomforts are symbolic of the disease in our life.

It's amazing how literal your body's messages can be. For instance, years ago when I quit a job I had for ten years to move to Ft. Lauderdale and start my own business, my right foot hurt for weeks. Once I got established with my new business my foot stopped hurting. It finally dawned on me -- I was worried about getting off on the right foot!!

I once heard about a teenager who was referred to a therapist by a doctor who couldn't find a medical reason why the young man was losing too much weight because he would choke up his food right after eating. During therapy sessions the boy shared with the psychologist the guilt he felt because he frequently masturbated. Although the boy said he shared his parents' and their fundamentalist church's beliefs in the evil of masturbation and sex only for procreation, he became so obsessed with a compulsion to masturbate that he couldn't swallow what he was doing! With therapy, this young man realized that he didn't have to accept all of his parents beliefs and came to his own conclusion that masturbation is not only normal but could be healthy. After that, the teenager not only kept his food down, but was no longer a compulsive masturbator.

Many times problems with the hands, including arthritis and rheumatism, may suggest the inability to handle certain situations. Another very interesting literal symbolism can be found in diabetes. My father died from diabetes at a young age after loosing his leg and having a stroke. Others in his family also had this disease. A common characteristic I observed among them was a lack of self-love or, if you will, a lack of sweetness. My dad ate for emotional fulfillment. This is also

31

true of many obese individuals who hide behind their weight and gorge themselves in order to feel loved. "Please give me some sugar!"

Many people who come to me for self-improvement and motivational classes think I'm psychic because I can tell them so much about their past, present and future by just looking at their bodies. For instance, if someone is wearing glasses I ask them if they started to wear glasses as a child. If they say yes, I ask them if there was a major conflict in their life at the time, especially a divorce. Many will recall what it was they <u>refused to see</u>. A child's vision may be temporarily impaired when there are events they don't want to see. If the event and the conflict were resolved first, the eyes would have adjusted themselves and the glasses might not have been needed.

Many asthmatic children I've worked with have highly overprotective parents, especially domineering mothers. Women who suffer from chronic fear and anxiety about the health of their baby even before the child is born, may end up smothering their children by being overly protective once the baby has arrived. And a child who has a medical condition is a constant concern to a parent. But children intuitively or unconsciously react to their parents' behaviors. I have one student who is fine when his mother is not around, but when his mother comes to pick him up you can see him tense up. She fusses around him and doesn't "let him breathe!"

And I have an adult student who has been able to isolate his attacks of asthma to times when his life is in crisis, especially during conflicts with his wife. He now understands that this is a throw back to the times his mother made him fearful about his condition by telling him, "Don't get upset, it will bring on an attack."

THE MORE WE ACCEPT, TRUST AND AFFIRM LIFE, THE DEEPER AND HEALTHIER WE BREATHE.

People who suffer from allergies present another good example of how we manifest emotional problems. Allergies are often a physical reaction to an emotional irritant. If you suffer from an allergic reaction, maybe you ought to ask the question, "Who am I allergic to?" It is not unusual for an "allergy" to clear up when a particularly disagreeable co-worker quits or after a divorce from the spouse we allow to "rub us the wrong way."

It is important to remember that we are all unique individuals and our bodies show the effects of stress in different ways. It does appear that there are common general diseases that are manifested similarly in the same manner. The contents of this chapter are based on my observations and my opinions. But I am not a physician or a psychologist. I tell students in my workshops and I recommend to you that you continue to see a medical doctor when necessary. But I also recommend that you examine your beliefs in relationship with your life objectively to see if you believe in what I call **BELIEFOLOGY**. If you do believe in the ability to create your reality, then I encourage you to create good health.

Your belief work may lead you to discover that one type of belief may affect more than one area of your life. For example, consider the scarcity belief, the belief that there is not enough to go around. I always associated prosperity and abundance -- or the lack of it -- with money and resources. I have improved my prosperity consciousness by getting in touch with my belief that there was never enough to go around. Although I have eliminated this erroneous belief in my financial area, I have discovered that this same erroneous belief is causing me some health challenges. I've always paced myself, limiting my activities for fear that I only have so much energy and unconsciously I have been creating a lack in my body by limiting oxygen intake as well as other vital nutrients necessary in maintaining optimal health. This belief has physically manifested in health problems.

Meanwhile, I have seen the opposite happen with one of my students. He improved his belief in the area of health only to manifest "lack" in his financial arena. As you go on to explore your root beliefs, watch to see if they crossover into more than one area so you can make conscious changes *wherever* they are needed.

Conscious Life Creations:
Money & Resources

Love, happiness, health and prosperity are the birthright of every creature -- human and animal. We must learn to claim our natural inheritance and attract to ourselves a sufficient amount of money and other resources to enable us to be free and fulfilled as opposed to the bondage of perpetual need and never having enough. The choice is yours. You can cultivate a prosperity consciousness so everything you touch, or invest energy in, reaps abundant results. You can have a poverty consciousness that perpetuates struggles, lack, and consequently, an unfulfilled life. There are four major core beliefs connected to abundance or poverty:

1. There's not enough to go around.
2. I don't deserve it nor do I feel worthy.
3. I don't have the skills or the ability.
4. Money is not spiritual and therefore is the root of all evil.

Currently the most prevalent belief is that of scarcities! This is an extremely erroneous and limiting belief! The universe is magnificently opulent and full of abundance! Just take a moment and try to comprehend the enormity of nature and the entire universe. Can you count the number of species of plants, animals and insects? How many life times would it take for you to visit all of the stars and planets in all the galaxies? Can you or anyone imagine the energy that could be constructively channeled from the sun and lightning! How many buckets of water would it take to hold all the rivers, lakes and oceans? And what about the universe's lifeblood -- oxygen? How much is there? *Where's the scarcity? What is* scarcity? It's in the mind and emotions and the poverty-consciousness of certain people, cities and countries. It's these continuous patterns of scarcity that create war and greed, and cause us to take more from nature than is required at given times. Scarcity drives individuals and corporations to stop at nothing to compete with others at any expense, and to hoard. When more people, as well as organizations, realize the true nature of the universe, you will see that the new world order will be one of cooperation versus vicious, vindictive, cut-throat competition. Furthermore, products and services will result in enhanced quality once this new way of life is accepted and implemented.

Deserving and worthiness are significant factors in determining whether or not a person has a prosperity consciousness. Without a strong self-esteem and belief in oneself it is extremely difficult to have feelings of worthiness. A lack of self-confidence will limit you in the area of skill development and you may hesitate to attempt to learn new trades or pursue academic challenges.

Another common belief is that life is a burden and the only way to make a living is to work hard and to struggle. Well-intended parents have passed down most of these beliefs. Always remember that there is no need to feel resentment towards your parents, for they raised you with the beliefs they blindly accepted from *their* parents. They may have been raised with a traditional work ethic that reinforced hard work, long hours and, in addition, promoted the concept of "no pain, no gain." This is not consistent with the natural laws of the universe, but many individuals misinterpret Eastern Religion by saying that desires are bad and the possession of material things is bad. How can desire be bad when it's desire that motivates consciousness to become all it can be while it expresses and experiences itself? It is my opinion that the originators of those old eastern religions suggested that the possession of material things could be limiting if you become too attached to them, allowing "things" or desires to own you. Therefore, you're never *free* to enjoy the fulfillment those "things" could provide because of struggling too much to let go and enjoy.

This becomes limiting because usually when you are attached to something that is old, outdated or no longer useful, you remain stuck with the old and will miss positive new opportunities. This can range from jobs, relationships, cars, clothes and homes, to belief systems and attitudes. Letting go of the old that no longer gratifies or provides a purpose is the pre-requisite for attracting the newly desired person, place or thing. The only things, thoughts or feeling that are truly beneficial to keep are those that are useful, positive and hold happy memories. As I stated earlier, your self-image will determine your future, so see yourself successful in the past, present and future and if you need to look back remember those beneficial choices that brought your favorite experiences. As for those unfavorable creations of the past, forgive yourself and let go. Live now, in the present moment, where your now and future is being created.

You may be asking yourself, "But shouldn't I be examining my past mistakes in order to identify and change my beliefs?" No. Actually you can do that in your current life's experiences. For instance, have you ever had this experience? You're paying your bills and your emotional, habitual response, including your self-talk, is frantically saying, "Oh, I never have enough left over for the extra things in life." Well, all of your beliefs and fears are accessible right then and can be replaced by trust, confidence and the realization that you can be a powerful receiver of all you need to enjoy a prosperous, rich life! If you were poor as a child, recall the feelings you had when on occasion you *felt* rich. Perhaps someone gave you an ice cream cone, a new dress outfit, or your family was invited to someone's Thanksgiving Feast! How did it make you feel?

Too many people focus on their bad luck, misfortune, or how little money, energy or time they have. Therefore, they are constantly reinforcing their "lack" image and will find it hard to escape this self-perpetuated bondage. Their words will be consistent, such as "I'm always broke," "There's never enough," "Right when I think I'm catching up," and on and on. Money is a symbol for an exchange of services or energy and it is neither good nor bad. Remember what I said earlier. Think of all the abundance in nature. We so often equate prosperity with money when money is only one form of abundance. Concentrate on and feel the money, time, resources and energy you have, even if it is only ten dollars.

Whenever you pay your bills, see and feel yourself as a partner of God, the universe, All That Is, (or whatever you want to call it), providing employment, enjoyment and education for all who are affiliated with whoever you're paying. In other words, when you pay your utility or grocery bills realize that you are assisting in financing the utility workers, or those store clerks, and benefiting each and every member of their families. The nature of the universe/God is to give. To withhold is to perish.

LIFE GIVES OF ITSELF IN ORDER TO LIVE.

As I observe the evolution of my prosperity consciousness I see a phenomenon I call the "spending/ debt margin of security". When I first set out to established credit, I thought a $300.00 line of credit was adequate. And when I borrowed that amount I felt like I was deep in debt! Now that I believe in my ability to earn a significantly higher income, I feel more comfortable owing more money. Financial security is relative. It's beneficial to affirm that your debts are proof that individuals or companies believe in your ability to earn the necessary income to pay what you owe. Still the spending "margin of security" should be the amount of money you feel *comfortable* spending.

For some people, there is too fine a line between their spending/debt margin of security and their scarcity or unworthiness beliefs that could lead to the reality of spending more than they take in. I stress that you *trust* -- trust in yourself and trust in the abundance of the universe. There is a natural, rhythmic flow of energy and money and your level of prosperity consciousness will determine the balance of the cycle of how much money is flowing in or out.

The theme of **BELIEFOLOGY** is to transform your beliefs and consequently change your consciousness. It's not that we don't have enough money, we need to enhance our prosperity consciousness. One of the most difficult hurdles for many of my students is the concept of receiving. Many are willing to give, give, give but are reluctant to receive, receive, receive. I've often said that if I stood downtown and passed out money, you would be surprised how many people would reject it. And so it is with life. So often life presents us with golden opportunities that we may pass by out of fear. You must become *open, receptive* vessels, willing and able to receive the abundance of an opulent, rich universe. *Life can only give you what you are willing to receive!* It's imperative to replace restrictive thought patterns and fearful emotional, habitual response patterns with new, healthy patterns that develop a new relationship with money. As I tell my students-- and life -- "I love money and money loves me." I'm not talking about the acquisition of money, but an unwavering trust and faith that you will always have whatever you need whenever you desire it to enjoy a fulfilling life on this planet.

Some other common affirmations regarding money are, "I always have more money coming in then going out." "I am a dynamic, powerful magnet attracting money, prosperity and abundance. Therefore I am happy, healthy and wealthy, and all is well in my reality!"

Surround your life with abundance. In order to change the thought patterns that transform your habitual emotional responses, *affirm* your new beliefs through your *every day actions* by gradually spending a few more dollars on a product of superior quality versus a generic brand, especially big-ticket items like a stereo or household furniture. Instead of buying something you feel is something you should settle for because it's cheap, wait until you have the money to buy that item you really want. You need to be the best, have the best and give the best. It's beneficial for you to give yourself permission to have what you want. "Go for the best and never settle for less."

Retrain your entire being towards quality. Can you imagine how productive, healthy and prosperous our world communities could be if everyone valued and honored their work, realizing their worth and always doing their best? When your self-talk responds with, "But who do you think you are?" please don't repress or deny that voice, but acknowledge that message and reply with," I am somebody that deserves and accepts the best life has to share." Instead of merely being a fundraiser in your daily pursuits to make a living, also be a friend raiser, especially being your own best friend. In addition, instead of purchasing one item at a time, buy several products when you go to the grocery. Gradually purchase several things you previously denied yourself. Take more time for yourself right now! Although you may currently be working many hours and return home to your spouse and children, inform them that you are taking at least a half hour to be alone and take a relaxing bubble bath or a walk. To ensure feelings of self-worth you must take more time for yourself, being kind and gentle. Furthermore, to enhance your prosperity consciousness, it's advantageous to appreciate the uniqueness and diversity of yourself and others as well as express gratitude and appreciation to yourself and to every person, creature and plant throughout the universe. To live a life of abundance and prosperity is to simultaneously celebrate not only your life but *all* life!

This is an area where I have made much progress. Initially, when I first realized and accepted the responsibility that everyone creates their life 100 %, I eagerly tried to change my life by utilizing the techniques of visualization and affirmation. It was like magic to see new relationships and job opportunities come into my life. Although I did not have a college degree, I nevertheless attracted jobs that required lots of responsibilities but because I didn't have a degree, I wasn't compensated like others doing a comparable job. Ever since I graduated from high school, I was committed to only working in jobs that were fun, unrestricted environments, where I had a valuable purpose, doing functional tasks. Unfortunately, none of them provided good monetary compensation. Finally after years of visualizing and affirming for prosperity, I found my reason for my lack of financial security. After doing intensive belief work I discovered it was an erroneous belief that I needed a college degree in order to get a fulfilling, purposeful job that paid adequately. So I said to myself, "Well obviously I'm half way there. I know I can attract a fulfilling job, but I need to replace the belief regarding the degree and sufficient compensation or I need to go back to college and 'earn' a degree."

Instead, I familiarized myself with the countless individuals throughout history who made significant contributions in many fields who never even finished elementary school and still found substantial positions and received generous payment. In addition to changing that belief, I worked on my worthiness and deserving beliefs. As I changed my beliefs I began to draw in employment opportunities that were classified as masters or Ph.D. level, and yes, with much higher salaries than I was accustomed to. I have had job offers from agencies and corporations throughout the country. Although they know I don't have a degree, they can see my successful track record. So you see, if you change your beliefs, you change your consciousness and automatically transform your life.

It has been extremely gratifying and fascinating to watch my students in self-improvement individual sessions and workshops transform their consciousness in the area of money. I can not tell you how many women who have come to me feeling they are trapped in either an unfulfilled marriage or even a battered relationship and would like to divorce but are fearful because of financial concerns. Surprisingly, many of the physically abused women were married to successful professionals, sometimes prominent figures in the community. Many of these individuals spent their lives after high school raising children so they never pursued a college education or a career. These women had the rigid belief that they had no skills and that it would be too late to gain skills because of their age. By using the "*BELIEFOLOGY*" concepts discussed in this book, I have assisted many of these women through their fear, trepidation and damaged self-esteem and they gradually changed their beliefs, took action, developed successful careers and left unhappy marriages to live newly beautiful, successful lives. While others continued with their old beliefs, and therefore continue to *feel* they are dependent on their husbands financially. These women have sentenced themselves in a prison-like life.

Another prevalent money belief is that making money isn't a problem, but keeping it is!! I met a man in one of my sessions in Fort Lauderdale, Florida who later contracted with me to provide consultation services to his magazine company. On several occasions this man secured millions of dollars from private investors for new ideas to develop new publications. However, each venture failed. Therefore it became beneficial for this man to identify the beliefs that were creating this pattern.

YOU CAN HAVE ALL THE MONEY IN THE WORLD,
BUT IF YOU DO NOT HAVE
A PROSPERITY CONSCIOUSNESS
THEN YOU WILL NOT CONTINUE
TO HAVE THE MONEY!

Just because you have the skills or a salable product, there's no guarantee of a life of prosperity. Consider all the great accomplished athletes who leave childhood homes of poverty to play for multi-million dollar contracts, only to end up eventually back in similar conditions. Yes, it's my theory that many successful athletes who feel unworthy or not deserving will draw to themselves either an injury or a disease to prevent them from being successful. Athletes who do not develop a prosperity consciousness usually "miss"-invest their money or will lose it one way or another. The same is true for many movie stars, rock stars and other entertainers who once lived a life of poverty and rose to fame and financial success only to later discover themselves in financial difficulties due to addictions, sickness, accidents or unwise investments. Or their beliefs might draw in either business or personal relationships with people who rob them of everything. Causation beliefs range from fear to not feeling worthy. But no matter what belief or combination of beliefs, there is something in their consciousness that is conversely opposed to financial success.

Review your beliefs in the area of money and resources and see if you can find your core beliefs. Remember your life is a mirror picturing your beliefs. If you're unsure of your beliefs *evaluate* the events occurring in your daily reality. Avoid judging because it will only set you back. Try to remember that you did the best you knew how to do.

Never compare yourself with others because we are all evolving in our own way at our own time. In addition the amount of money a person needs is relative to what that person needs to fulfill his or her life purpose. To develop and maintain a life of abundance for yourself, it's imperative that you cultivate your personal life organization as a *FOR-PROFIT* agency verses a *NOT-FOR-PROFIT* reality. In the end, your inner self-worth will determine your financial net worth.

Conscious Life Creations:
Personality, Character/Self-Esteem

A healthy personality, strong value-based character, and powerful self-esteem is at the center and foundation of *BELIEFOLOGY.*

Probably the most important characteristic that has been lacking in our society is personal responsibility. The reason I named my company Individual Growth & Fulfillment was to address and meet the needs of individuals. In the last several years there has been increased focus on family and community. But without self-directed and self-responsible individuals, you cannot have a healthy family or community. Society is an ecosystem that requires an interdependent balance that can only come about with an understanding and acceptance of how everyone relates and is affected by everyone and everything else. Most of the decay, deterioration, illness, distraction, hatred, greed, poverty and crime of today are all symptoms and results of *powerlessness.* Emphasis on self-esteem and teaching individuals the importance of being motivated and self-responsible can help to overturn these conditions.

Most of our current institutions, including the justice system, medicine, military, education, organized religions, governments and business have their framework, foundation and essential structure centered in an outdated, authoritarian belief system. This collective belief system is founded on the survival of the fittest mentality (Darwin's evolutionary theory); limiting religious indoctrination, including original sin; Freudian psychology; medical theories based on curing disease rather than preventing it; authoritative child raising; and an educational system with a curriculum driven by memorizing facts and too much emphasis on grades and degrees. Our entire framework has been built from an extremely weak, negative, limiting paradigm, or set of rules. We have come to accept that our bodies are vulnerable to outside enemies such as germs, we must protect ourselves against the communists, we must spank kids in order for them to obey authority, and essentially that we'd better not trust anybody. What a life! No wonder so many people live in a *fearful* world full of hate, war and disease with people willing to control and step on others to get what they want.

Through the lessons to be learned in *BELIEFOLOGY,* you can start to build new paradigms based on natural laws to replace those old historical structures that we have all *acquiesced* to collectively. The outdated framework created by male-dominated cultures and maintained by control through fear and the perpetuation of the concept of reward and punishment, good and bad, and right and wrong needs to be changed. Most of the beliefs are unnatural and man-made and have been passed down by many generations. In most cases they have never been examined objectively. It's important for each *individual* to examine his/her beliefs and release those that no longer serve them. The new, natural laws that are a part of many new paradigms are creating major new shifts in many organizations, philosophies, and, yes, even in science, governments, medicine and religion. This new evolution realizes that we are all a part of God, and therefore each creature, including man, is intrinsically good, powerful, loving, healthy, motivated by basic good intent and is interconnected with an abundant, powerful, resourceful universe. They recognize that the universe, God, ALL THAT IS, or whatever you want to name it, is always for YOU! Or as a friend of mine says, "The universe is bent in your direction."

Now what does this have to do with you as an individual and your personality, character and self-esteem? Let's look at each of the paradigms, comparing the old with the new, and see the effects both can have on your development.

45

THE JUDICIAL SYSTEM

The judicial system is pretty self-explanatory. It is based on right/wrong and punishment. The premise is that you can't trust all the people because some are good and some are bad, and therefore laws and regulations must be created to insure order. Of course, good and bad have always been relative and changes to meet the prejudices of the times. For example, at one time in some places in our country, a black person drinking out of a "white drinking fountain" was considered bad, even illegal. Now there are no such laws.

The deterrent to crime has always been thought to be punishment. Most of society believes the solution to today's problems is to "make a law". These are man-made laws. Yet despite new laws being created each year, crime, assaults, child abuse and spouse abuse continues to increase. Maybe it's the good/bad, reward/punishment mentality that is creating the problem. From this framework of reward and punishment has come the concept known as GUILT! And whenever we feel guilty about something, we attract a punishment.

The premise of **BELIEFOLOGY** is clear on this issue:

YOU CREATE YOUR LIFE
ACCORDING TO YOUR BELIEFS!

If you accept this as a universal natural law, then you see that there can be no victims. I'm not saying we should do away with all the man-made laws. At this time in history, without them the world would experience total chaos because so many people aren't self-directed or personally responsible. Of course, we will always need man-made systems, structures, and laws that are for our convenience, such as traffic regulations and procedural processes. But the only way our society will achieve it's family and community values, as well as all of the new paradigm shifts in organization, is through the <u>REVOLUTION</u> of the <u>INDIVIDUAL</u> and his/her entire <u>PSYCHE</u>!

BUSINESS AND INDUSTRY

Historically, the industrial age encouraged organizational and economic systems to mold and manipulate men and women to meet its institutional needs. To accomplish this, companies would utilize coercive, dogmatic methods of fear and punishment that often generated as much hostility as it did productivity. Furthermore, this process repressed, depressed and suppressed an employee's natural creativity and his/her drive to come up with alternative solutions to problems that could have increased the company's profits.

This work environment based on reward/punishment often led to rebellion by the work force that gave the institutions the notion that even more force and control were necessary. The needs of the individual were sacrificed for the benefit of the authoritarian system. Only when individuals can develop a true sense of determination and their own self-worth can there be a real sense of family/community values, harmony and joint economic prosperity.

✠ ✠ ✠ ✠

Another shift in values, thoughts and perceptions come from the transition from the Industrial Era that profited from rigid hierarchies, production lines, centralized operations and one-job careers, to the Information Age, characterized by global economy, flexibility, cooperation, interdependence, self regulation and sophisticated technology. Previously our value, security and identity were dependent upon our employment position. Future jobs will be determined by a person's purpose, skills and intent. This will result in a win-win situation for both employer and employee. With innovations in technology along with major downsizing in private and government operations, millions of workers will be laid off around the world. However, entrepenurism will come into its own during the next ten years. The true measure of this change relies on the personal responsibility, confidence and self-esteem of each individual. Thus the independence created will eliminate the need for the old authority structures of business and government. The results will not only be favorable for the individual but will be productive financially, culturally and in every way collectively. Instead of an individual losing his/her uniqueness, organizations and governmental systems will actually serve the people. Only then will we truly see interdependence.

HEALTH AND HUMAN SERVICES

Human Services and medicine also have their roots immersed in a fear and authoritarian- driven paradigm. Clearly the new health paradigm, as discussed earlier in this book, has its focus on the body's biological integrity and it's propensity towards natural self-healing. Historically there was a concentration on the fear of disease, with the idea that our weak bodies had to be protected at all cost from illness and bad health. People were taught to protect themselves from germs and viruses, and that collective inoculations were imperative. The medical community reinforced the powerlessness of the individual and convinced the masses that the only hope for good health came from an outside authority healer -- the medical physician and his medicine. However the new paradigm places its emphasis on health and is gradually replacing the sickness model.

Individuals are coming to realize that an outside agent such as a doctor or medicine may assist in their healing, however the healing process also consists of self-healing. You can help figure out the cause of your imbalances and make adjustments to correct them via changes in your thinking, beliefs and life style.

The physical body is merely a reflection of the emotional body. Medical pioneers like Deepak Chopra and Bernie Siegal are helping individuals to reclaim their natural power and take responsibility for their own health and happiness.

HEALTH AND HAPPINESS IS THE NATURAL STATE OF OUR BODY.

Unlike the old paradigms, illness is not something thrust upon you but a natural communication -- or as I say a "biological barometer" -- that is informing you that something is out of balance in your life.

ﱠ ﱠ ﱠ ﱠ

Other medical practices that have added to the fearful, authoritarian paradigm are in the fields of psychology and psychiatry. So much of our current education on child rearing, social interrelationships, business and personal sense of self have been influenced by behaviorist psychology. The emphasis on lengthy psychoanalysis and the powerless conscious mind implies that we are victims of our contaminated subconscious. Furthermore, behaviorism reinforces the reward and punishment phenomenon that not only creates rigid structures, but also perpetuates more guilt and anxiety.

Professionals in the fields of psychology and psychiatry could be the greatest catalyst to transforming our society. Once they accept the mind-body connections and the implications of creating our own reality, they can assist individuals in changing their beliefs. They will help to reverse those worn out limiting beliefs of the shameful, frightened collective self-image, and

49

repudiate the flawed self-image that comes from the weak, guilt-ridden self-pictures from a warped sub-conscious. Less emphasis will be placed on victimhood and going to childhood to find causes. New successes will be discovered by acting on the "point of power" in the moment and the power of the present, conscious mind.

MILITARY

The institution that has created the most destruction, tears, pain and futile bleeding is the military. This institution is the outward manifestation of our fearful, insecure personal structure. So many wars have been fought to protect land in the name of God or patriotism and other prejudices. With the development of mass communication, mass travel and a breaking down of prejudice, we will no longer have these tribal turfdom issues.

War gives individuals who have built up an accumulation of hate -- culminating with a lack of purpose -- an opportunity to release this hostility in a socially accepted way. In fact, many war heroes were motivated and given a reason to live because they were able to vent their unnatural aggression. Students studying past decades will be saddened that so much of the indoctrination toward the fear of communism, atheists, and other evils on the list, was actually driven by economic factors along with the need for groups to maintain control of their self-interests.

In addition, many wars are the result of a "scarcity belief" -- whether it's a scarcity of money, land or natural resources. Once humans realize we live in a prosperous universe there will be no need for greed and war. As we unite with other nations in the collaboration of a global economy the incidence of war should diminish.

EDUCATION

Our educational system is based on curriculums designed to memorize facts and classroom discipline that demands obedience to authority. The future educational system will be much more individualized, based on the premise that children have a natural desire to learn, and that they are curious, creative and naturally cooperative. It will be widely recognized that *every person* is unique, with a life purpose that will not only fulfill them personally but also contribute to all of humanity. Children have a built-in potential, with all the needed skills and talents to achieve this purpose. Believe it or not, we are a part of creaturehood and just as the tulip bulb has within it all the potential to be a colorful flower, each child has its physical, mental and emotional characteristics' prerequisites inherent within. Therefore, the function of education should be to facilitate, nurture and cultivate a child's curiosity and natural propensity towards the *process* of learning.

Education will be a preparation for the new world, where everyone is responsible, powerful, sensitive, knowledgeable and able to utilize the new sophisticated computerized technologies.

Perhaps the most significant transformation in education will be in the area of self-esteem. Students will be encouraged to cultivate their intuitive/psychic development; and they will be encouraged to be self-directed and to be problem-solvers. Our society does not encourage uniqueness -- the idea that it is okay to be original or different. Actually we promote conformity. This trend motivates some children to steal $100.00 gym shoes they can't otherwise afford in order to be one of the crowd. It also stimulates peer-pressure to enter the world of chemical addiction, whether it's smoking, alcohol or drugs.

Many children, and adults, don't have a purpose or feel they don't have the ability to make a significant contribution to the world. In other words, they don't feel they count. Along with purpose, education needs to teach choice making. Hopefully schools will teach subjects like **BELIEFOLOGY**, to reveal to students that they do not have to suffer and struggle like previous generations. Parents have always wanted their children to have a better life, and of course, all generations did the best they could within the framework of their own limiting mass beliefs. If schools would teach and promote self-esteem, which includes unconditional love and belief in self and cooperation with others, there could be a significant reduction in addictions and an increase in well-being and productivity. One of the most important reasons we live is to be happy, yet so many of our life-patterns are contrary to this. Perhaps we need to teach how to choose happiness, and to avoid or reverse old patterns that perpetuate unhappiness.

This holistic approach to education must take into account not only the *individual* person, but also his/her interdependence within the entire universe. The new educational system will collaborate and plan its curriculums to meet the needs of the public/private sector and their growing changes. *The new discoveries with quantum physics and progress with computers and electronics will literally transform all segments of our world and consequently education!* In fact don't be surprised to see in addition to the outer-space program, the creation of an inner-space program. Once modern physicists prove their new theories, physicians, religious leaders and scientist will finally relinquish old dogma and will work cooperatively to promote the understanding of the inter-connectivity of all beings and things. They will ultimately realize and accept that they were limiting themselves by perceiving/studying *parts* of life instead of the whole that includes the physical as well as the metaphysical. An important part of the non-physical is feelings like unconditional love, happiness, fulfillment and unconditional acceptance. As we "un-teach" ourselves the erroneous things we learned in the past, we need to say "no" to unhappiness and start to live to our fullest potential.

Another way to enhance positive personality character/self-esteem is to integrate child-raising with education. The less erroneous beliefs your children learn when they're young, the fewer they will have to "un-learn" when they are older.

In our culture it is common for young women to have children in order to fill a void or lack of purpose in their life or raise their own self-esteem. TV talk shows feature young girls -- and boys -- who express a desire to have babies in order to have someone to love them. Often these young parents project their unhealthy belief system on to their children, and it becomes a repetitive cycle.

Other talk shows cover stories about young children, especially girls, who think they are too fat. These are children, as young as five years old, who are obsessed with weight to the extent of counting calories and fat! Statistics show that 1 out of every 3 adolescent girls are on a rigid diet because they feel they are fat. Should this really surprise us in a society that is so glamour and appearance oriented? This attitude carries over into adulthood. How many people do you know whose happiness is contingent on their waist size or the number that registers on their bathroom scale? How many parents do you know who push and pressure their children to excel in academics, athletics or beauty pageants to compensate for what they feel they missed as a child, or even to build up their own recognition in the community? Are they allowing their children to be children? And what does this teach children about self-esteem?

BELIEFOLOGY is based on the theory that children are born with a curious nature, with the desire to explore, seeking and enjoying pleasure, living in the here and now and instinctively following their impulses. Observe children at play. They greet each day with enthusiasm, joy and energy, in a quest for life, knowing and living unconditional love. But over the years adults learn to repress, suppress and depress all of these natural characteristics. It starts with the young child whose hand gets slapped if he/she is caught exploring his/her body, as if their sexual organs were evil. Children are sent to schools to learn how to stand in straight lines, or ask permission to speak or go to the bathroom. Children are taught not to be independent thinkers and are often led away from listening to their impulses by a society that believes the influence of demons will lead them astray.

Young children -- with their free spirits -- are "taught" to deny their instincts, delay or prohibit their pleasure and to deny the natural feelings that could lead to health, abundance, happiness and personal responsibility. The new paradigm regarding child rearing will focus on acceptance, love, nurturing, personal responsibility and cultivating a healthy strong sense of self and a powerful self-esteem. The new replacement for the old educational system will teach children that they are not enclosed in their bodies -- that they are *more* than their bodies -- and will help them to learn to access the powers of the mind, attracting positive events through being and accepting the natural self and cooperating with others instead of the ruthless competition that breeds greed, jealousy and hatred.

I'm not advocating that we be a permissive society, but one that exemplifies, as well as expects, personal responsibility. Children can be taught to be inner-directed and motivated accordingly, based on preferences that benefit the individual as well as the community instead of the former framework of outer-directions based on reward and punishment. Instead of punishment, parents can teach children about natural consequences and teach responsible choice making. Outer rewards will lose importance when children realize that all real peace, happiness and fulfillment come from within! Furthermore, they will understand the universal laws of cause and effect and realize that when they harm another human being or mother nature there will most likely be an equivalent, unfavorable event or experience to greet them later. In addition to learning how to make discerning choices, children will learn how to engage in *mutual, natural, honest* communication -- with themselves as well as others.

We can enhance a child's *ZEST* for life by facilitating opportunities for growth, exploration and fulfillment. Parents should not have children to meet their own needs, but must first *love themselves*, and be prepared to teach by example once they bring children into the world. Mothers and fathers can share unconditional love through gentle nurturing, and can teach children that there is great strength in gentleness.

The new way of raising future responsible adults will center around establishing a safe, loving, accepting, empowering environment that encourages self-expression, self-responsibility, belief in self, and the unconditional acceptance of self. With this foundation, children will find it easier to accept and appreciate their own uniqueness and embrace the uniqueness and diversity of their fellow brothers and sisters.

RELIGION

The most dramatic and controversial shift in world views to influence an individual's personality, character and self-esteem is the ongoing transformation of religions. Historically, religions have been based on the belief in a paternal God who was usually portrayed as judgmental, sometimes vengeful, wrathful, periodically benevolent and always separate from "his" creations. Western Christian philosophy preaches that you are born in sin, and that you need to be baptized and accept Christ as your personal savior in order to escape from a descent into eternal hell. Combine this religious hierarchical patriarchy with the influence of scientists who proclaim the universe was a meaningless accident, and add a controlling male government ruled by an economy that is driven by ruthless competition and the need to win at any cost and maybe you can understand why humans feel powerless, fearful, without purpose, possessing a low self-esteem.

The human consciousness is in need of some balancing. We must integrate more feminine characteristics, such as nurturing, love, gentleness, compassion, intuition and forgiveness. In the last several years, there's been a search and hunger for this lack and people have begun resurrecting old Eastern and Native American religions and philosophies. In addition, there has been an increased interest in the Goddess religions.

As an outcome of the woman's lib movement of the sixties, men and women are becoming more androgynous. Consequently this is being reflected in the collective psyche and will affect the way we think, feel, live and do business. As this evolves and we include more feminine principles into our daily lives, the old controlling male authoritarian institutions will begin to change. Our culture will move away from traditional religious rituals and dogma to a nature-oriented spirituality that will be expressed in a more natural and spontaneous manner. Fewer people will attend church. They will prefer a more private, personal relationship with their God spirit, communing with a God that is perceived as a life force within everything instead of outside and separate from them. Future churches will be based less on symbolism and will take more of a teaching role, leaving ritual and ceremony only for the celebration of life. Once this transformation takes place and the old institutions are replaced with the new way of thinking, feeling and living, then each individual will be self-actualized with a strong character and self esteem that will be reflected in the greater community where people will live in harmony within a prosperous, powerful and vibrant universe.

Conscious Life Creations:
Relationships

By now you have had an opportunity to uncover some of your beliefs that you may have not been aware of previously. You may have found several erroneous beliefs that bleed through from one area of your life to another. For example you may have a belief that you're not worthy or deserving. Not only does this affect your ability to make money, but it may also interfere with attracting or maintaining a harmonious relationship.

Try this exercise. Write several paragraphs describing your ideal relationship with the following: self, siblings, parents, friends, co-workers, community and God (universal intelligence, ALL THAT IS, cosmic consciousness or whatever you call it). If your parents are no longer on this side of life, use your imagination and describe the ideal relationship you would have preferred unless the remembered memory is the ideal.

Now list the differences between your preferred ideal relationship and those of your current relationship. What possible beliefs, both positive and negative, may have created your present relationship? Examine those beliefs. Affirm and strengthen the favorable beliefs while accepting and releasing those beliefs that are not beneficial. Always remember there is a time lapse between our thoughts and the subsequent manifestation of that electromagnetic energy.

YOUR PRESENT REALITY IS THE PRODUCT OF YOUR THOUGHTS, DREAMS, BELIEFS AND EXPECTATIONS OF YESTERDAY AND THE BELIEFS OF TODAY WILL CREATE YOUR REALITY FOR YOUR FUTURE.

The awareness of this concept is essential in attracting positive and harmonious relationships.

I can't count the number of students who requested individual sessions with me to discuss their personal mission to find a significant relationship. After having experienced a failed relationship, people go out searching for Mr. or Miss Right, only to draw in a similar relationship, attracting someone with the same characteristics as their past partners. My advice is always the same -- before committing to anything serious you may (its always free choice) consider doing some belief work. Examine and, if needed, transform any beliefs you have regarding self-identity, self-esteem, deservability, self-confidence and most important, self-love. As one of my spiritual teachers, Amel, often states, "In essence the only lesson there is is Self." This upsets some people because they feel this is an extremely selfish attitude. But in relationship to *BELIEFOLOGY*, this makes a lot of sense. Your beliefs, attitudes and emotions contribute to composing your consciousness and it's your consciousness that determines your daily life. So it's only natural to realize that the exploration and acceptance of self is imperative. Only through realizing and accepting who and what you are now, and by finding that inner love, strength, trust and intimacy with self can you learn to trust and be intimate with others.

For some time now there have been social diseases running rampant in our society with many names like codependency, neediness, battered spouse abuse, child abuse and addictions. Our music and movies and television programs continue to reinforce the following beliefs: "I'm nothing without you." "I need you." "I love you more than life itself." "I can't live without you." "I will kill you if you leave me." "You make me jealous." "If you cheat on me I will kill you." And these are just a few!

There are many people (especially women) who allow their partners to beat them physically or abuse them emotionally. The common response from these "victims" when asked why they stay is usually, "But I love him (her)!" One of the most important themes in *BELIEFOLOGY* is *"There are NO VICTIMS".* Every person you draw into your life is there for a purpose -- to enjoy, to help you learn and grow, and to act as a mirror to reflect the image of yourself and how you perceive yourself, God and life.

Essentially all of these social diseases are co-created because people *want to be loved, wanted and validated.* The root of all of these addictions is *the constant struggle to be accepted/approved and valued.* We need to evolve in our conscious awareness of our innate divinity and power to become more self-accepting, self-appreciating, and self-loving, while we simultaneously develop an intimate relationship with ourselves, enjoying, expressing and sharing all that we are. Unfortunately, there are those people who feel a void. They feel as though they are half a person who needs somebody or something (addiction) to somehow fill the missing half or void. If you find a person or discover a remedy (addiction), I can assure you it will be temporary, because the illusion will end and until you become a whole person within yourself, you will be doomed to repeat/attract over and over again pain, struggle, conflict, guilt and distress.

LIKE CONSCIOUSNESS ATTRACTS LIKE CONSCIOUSNESS.

Usually one of four things occurs after the break-up of a detrimental relationship. You will:
1. Have difficulty attracting a new relationship or choose not to ever have relationships fearing the possibilities;
2. Feel desperate and lonely and would rather be with the familiar, abusive partner instead of developing

self-worth and waiting for the best relationship to find you;

3. Rush into a new relationship only to discover that the person has more or less the same personality traits as your former abusive partner, or the new person is similar to an abusive parent;

4. Rush into another relationship for the sake of security or out of neediness, instead of concentrating on learning how to accept, love, forgive and believe in self.

Introduce yourself to yourself and maybe for the first time in your life ask:

- Who am I?
- What makes me happy?
- What is my life purpose?
- What sort of life style do I want?
- What type of people and relationships can I really have once I really know I'm worthy and it's my natural inheritance to have the best relationships?

There is no reason to become a recluse or take up celibacy during your transitional self-growth period. Learn to become friends with members of the opposite sex. You may or may not engage in enjoyable sex without losing yourself or making commitments until you become a whole person, ready to attract the best relationship. It's often beneficial to date many people to learn more about yourself, as well as enhancing your realization that there are a lot of interesting people offering lots of opportunities. Try not to place too much emphasis on good looks. So often people will limit themselves by wanting someone pretty or handsome, and after committing to a relationship will discover that although the outside may be appealing, the inside (personality) is not, and consequently in time the outer appearance may not be so attractive.

Perhaps the most challenging part of creating your own reality is accepting the idea that no matter how much you love your friends or relatives, and although they may give you advice, suggestions and support, only *you* can change your consciousness.

LIFE IS A DO-IT-YOURSELF PROJECT!

Of course, this works in reverse. You may recognize the erroneous beliefs of friends or relatives that keep drawing the unpleasant events and disease into their lives, but they have to take responsibility for their own lives and transform their own consciousness. Until they do, there is absolutely nothing you can do except love and accept them unconditionally. It's easier for a "victim" to blame parents, associates, society and circumstances than to take responsibility to make different choices and decisions.

Besides your beliefs, your life is the culmination of all the choices and decisions you've ever made. It's difficult enough to identify what it is *you* really believe and subsequently change *your* emotional responses when you take responsibility. Know you have the power to create your life. Although most people want to be healthy and happy, there are those individuals who enjoy conflict, disease and unhappiness and will sabotage any possibilities of happiness. Unhappiness, anger and conflict are just as much a choice to be made as is happiness. It's nearly impossible to maintain positive relationships with friends, co-workers and relatives without conflict if you do believe in victimhood and you continue to make choices that will perpetuate trends and patterns of conflict, unhappiness, sickness and even emotional and physical abuse.

While you are embarking upon this journey of creating a new, positive, healthy, prosperous and joyful life experience, don't give up until you gradually manifest your new mental blue prints. In an earlier chapter we talked about your inner-self, via electromagnetic vibrations, acting as a casting studio that selects actors and actresses that match your chosen life's script according to your beliefs, emotions and expectations. This is where timing and synchronization come into play. Let me illustrate this process with two *hypothetical* situations.

Probability I: Susan was raised with several different step-fathers and had a tendency to attract men with similar characteristic as each of these parents. In relationships, she would always assume a subservient role and seldom felt worthy of pursuing her personal choices. Therefore, Susan attracted extremely domineering men who periodically *physically* abused her and often *emotionally* abused her. There was always a part of Susan that recognized her patterns and realized that there was a stronger but repressed personality that she wanted to express. So she goes to the bookstore and purchases a copy of **BELIEFOLOGY** and invests a lot of time and effort in belief work in order to attract and maintain a harmonious relationship.

Simultaneously, in another part of the city, there is a man we will call Harry, who is extremely disillusioned with his marriage. This man initially was happy in his marriage. But he had married at a young age, and he matured and now has different interests than his wife. In time he is able to convince his wife it would be advantageous for both of them if they end their marriage and start new lives. They agree to divorce in six months once his wife completes her college degree.

Now, with that background, we have Susan visualizing a new relationship with the intent to draw into her life a relationship based on her new beliefs. While Susan is sleeping, her dream-self searches the vacancies located at the collective inner-selves casting studio. Likewise, Harry, during his dream state, solicits his intent for a new relationship, and his dream-self and Susan's dream-self conduct a co-interview.

Meanwhile, during her awake reality, Susan feels alive with her new transformed consciousness. She has been dating several men and all of them want to make a commitment. However, although she is happy and satisfied with these men, Susan's intuition is urging her to wait and she doesn't know why. Seven months later she is on her way home from work and her little voice sends her a very loud message: "Stop at that corner neighborhood bar that has always been intriguing." Although her mother had died several years ago her mom's voice echoes in Susan's mind, commanding her not to stop there. "Nice women never go into bars alone because men aren't any good and they are only after one thing." In a quandary Susan drives into the parking lot and decides to follow her impulse.

Susan enters the bar and takes a seat in the eating section of the bar. Still uncomfortable with her decision, she almost dashes out of the bar until she happens to glance at a near- by booth and notices a man reading a book. Could it be? The book happens to be *BELIEFOLOGY*. She initiates a conversation and discovers that this man attends a weekly class on this subject matter. He invites her to attend a class. Finally the two became intimate and chose to share a permanent relationship that is mutually harmonious, fulfilling and beneficial. Yes, the man is Harry who is by now divorced from his wife.

Probability II: Imagine the same scenario as Probability I. Harry agrees to stay with his wife for six months while she earns her degree. Meanwhile, Susan, not consciously knowing anything about the "chance" encounter with Harry, pushes events and marries another man before the end of the 6 months. Susan never meets Harry. Instead Susan attracts a better relationship than she had, but not as harmonious or fulfilling as the relationship she could have had with Harry.

There are three major lessons to be learned from these two hypothetical probabilities. First, they present an example of how changing your beliefs can consequently transform your consciousness and this can reveal itself in your relationships. Second, they illustrate the synchronicity of events and the time lapse between when you change your mental atmosphere (consciousness) and when it subsequently begins to appear in your physical atmosphere. Oftentimes we do not trust in our abilities to attract new experiences so we push events and unfortunately settle for better instead of best. And third, they emphasize the importance of following your intuition. We've been taught not to be impulsive. Nevertheless, one of the foundations of the concept of *BELIEFOLOGY* is to become inner-directed and that it is beneficial to listen and act upon your natural impulses. Your intuition is one of the most direct messengers and conduits that connect you with your higher self and your divine connection with ALL THAT IS, Universal Intelligence or what ever you refer to as God. If Susan refused to respond to her intuition in Probability I and didn't stop at the bar, chances are she would not have been at the right place at the right time and her life would have been so different. So you can see the importance of selecting your choices and how frequently one simple choice can impact thousands of lives. Ask your co-workers and friends how they and their parents met their mates and you will see how a choice creates probabilities that create children and their children, all due to being at the right place at the right time.

The androgynous revolution that started in the sixties will culminate with the integration of the male and female aspects within us. This process is imperative because only when you fill in your gaps and become whole, mature and balanced can you share a relationship with another who has also become whole and balanced. As we do this collectively, we create a healthy community, and the well-being of our world and society as well.

As stated in earlier chapters, our present institutions were built from a world view whose archetypal psyche consisted of masculine dominance. This over-identification with the masculine has resulted in an unbalanced culture and is responsible for many of our social ills as well as being the significant cause of problems in relationships with self and others. This has led to negation, denial, suppression and repression of feminine principles. Principles/Characteristics have created our competitive "win/lose" business and academic paradigms, nurturing greed, violence, strife, even war. Have you ever thought about the shape of a bullet, missile or rocket? Isn't it symbolic of the male penis? We have devalued feminine characteristics that create the natural world like intuition, love, emotions, body sexuality, dreams, relatedness and receptivity. It is essential for men to claim their feminine qualities and for women to reclaim their own feminine, as well as masculine qualities. When this happens, we will see collectively new paradigms of unconditional love, cooperation and natural prosperity replace old, out-dated masculine institutions.

As we merge into a new world, we will become more aware of the fact that we are not enclosed in our bodies and that we are divine spirits of love and power; co-creatures with father-mother God. The more we express our unique God-hood, the more we will expand and enhance our newly developed relationships built on self-confidence, worthiness and trust. And we will extend the same opportunities of freedom to others. As we cultivate this beautiful divine love affair with ourselves, "turfdom" issues will finally come to an end. Most of our historical wars have been over territory or religion. We will learn to accept and be tolerant of the unique differences in our selves and others, and outgrow homophobias and other bigoted behavior. The major transformation will culminate when human beings realize that they are not separate from God but partners -- a part of the same source of power, beauty, love and truth. On an individual basis, as well as collectively, there is an evolution towards freedom. We are breaking down barriers ranging from government, science, religion and self-inflicted boundaries in order to enjoy the natural freedom of life!

So the catalyst for this new emergence of the awareness of cosmic "beingness" will be the new relationship with self and the cultivation of a new realization and relationship with God. The prerequisite to the activation of this partnership with God is the awakening of you within this divine essence, with the awareness and acceptance of the power and energy that flows through everything you are and do. You need to reclaim your power and recognize the strength in gentleness. Accept your inner authority and exemplify your new relationship with the universe by expressing honor, integrity, joy, peace and unconditional love. As for masculine characteristics, females need to embrace and activate strength and power. Man needs to realize and reclaim true natural power and understand that natural power has nothing to do with control or hostile aggression. Humans too often equate power with negative associations. Poverty, anger, fear, hate, guilt, limitation, violence, anger, isolation and disease are all manifestations of powerlessness.   Only through the expression of life from a universal power from the divine source within can you overcome powerlessness.

Most of the problems and conflicts in our relationships are caused when we choose to give away our power. *No one can make us angry, jealous, unhappy or fearful. We allow others to have power over us.* Remember, you choose your thoughts and your emotional responses are created by those beliefs.   You relinquish your power by requiring outer-validation and approval from other people including your partner.   Guilt, anger and jealously are products of fear, inadequacy, lack of self-confidence and powerlessness.

Healthy, harmonious living and happy relationships exist when two balanced, whole, self-actualized/fulfilled individuals share with each other but remain independently strong. If you are currently involved in a successful relationship, it's still beneficial to create space for yourself within the relationship. Make time to be alone and separate from your partner and to nourish your own spirit so if the time comes that you do not want to be together anymore, you will have no fear of being by yourself.

It's been my experience that many women, especially from older generations, stayed in unhappy (sometimes abusive) marriages not only for financial reasons, but also because of the fear of being by themselves. During one on-going class my students were doing some belief work and visualization in tandem and one woman chose to visualize her husband being attracted to another woman and asking her for a divorce. I suggested that it might be timely for her to become more assertive and for *her* to ask her husband for the divorce since she was unsatisfied. However, she didn't want to hurt him, and do you know what happened? The visualization worked. Three months later her husband engaged in an affair with a co-worker and revealed it to his wife. The couple discussed their deepest feelings and desires for the first time. The marriage ended but the discussions resulted in a mutual friendship that never existed during the marriage. When you truly love someone unconditionally, you want them to be happy even if it means releasing your loved one if they choose to move on in life without you. If you truly love and believe in yourself, you will not enter into the fear of jealousy because you will sincerely know that you have much to offer and can attract another relationship. You are totally self-sufficient, so believe in YOU!

The foundation of **BELIEFOLOGY** is that you create your reality according to your beliefs and the realization that there are no victims or accidents. In our daily lives we project our fears and self-judgments. If you are being judgmental or being non-forgiving of others, you are essentially judging yourself and not willing to forgive yourself. If you agree with the premise of creating your personal reality, it's advantageous for you to learn how to forgive others. Revenge, hate and hostile feelings don't hurt the people they are directed at as much as they limit you and create self-stress and conflict. Release your resentments and recriminations and you will discover that into your life will come more health, happiness, prosperity and positive relationships. The same goes for guilt, another product of anger and fear. When you take full responsibility and complete ownership of your life, you no longer need those useless emotions that limit your life. When you live from that point of power, you can break the cycle of attraction that maintained the old, undesirable conditions.

Symbolically you can assist a change in your consciousness by cleaning out your closets, drawers, garage, cabinets and your house. Throw out, or even better, give away things and clothes that no longer serve you. Doing this in tandem with clearing your mind of limiting beliefs and attitudes makes room in your consciousness, and consequently, in your life for the new!!

∾ ॐ ∾ ॐ

Earlier in this book I defined all matter as awarized energy with certain degrees of consciousness. This energy culminates synergistically with vibrating light and sound. The vibrations occur so fast that it gives an illusionary appearance of solid, consistent matter. We also discussed the interconnection of all things, including creaturehood and the physical world. Well there are relationships between your energy and the energy of your household appliances, your automobile and other electrical or mechanical things. Although I plan to write a book solely on this subject, I want to briefly explain how this connection is relevant to relationships and how we do indeed create our reality. The following are a few examples:

Illustration 1. I had a student in Fort Lauderdale who called one day to tell me she was running late for her individual session because her car overheated. She had just left the courthouse where she had finalized her divorce settlement. She was extremely angry. In fact, to quote her, she was "boiling" because in her opinion her husband had a better lawyer and she felt she had received an unfair settlement. In her individual session we discussed the possibilities that created the event. Her car was fairly new and she never had a problem before. Could her radiator have been affected by her anger?

Illustration 2. For a period in 1983, I was in a quandary, trying to decide if and when I should leave my full-time job to pursue self-employment. During that period of time I went through four starters on my car. Three of them failed after several months and another one had manufacturing defects. Once I made a decision and felt comfortable with my time line for leaving my job, I never had a problem with a starter on that or any future car. Was this reflecting my procrastination and inability to start my new job/life?

Illustration 3. A counselor was holding sessions at her home and although her house was only a year old, the drains, including her toilet started to clog. Were her clients leaving their "shit" at her house?

Illustration 4. For months a student expressed frustration and anxiety because he was being "bugged" by his ex-wife, co-workers, and certain neighbors. Then all in a period of one week he informed me that he had an infestation of ants at home and personally he had head lice he believed might have been transferred by a co-worker. Were the bugs a physical manifestation reflection of his mental/emotional state of feeling "bugged"? And to remedy the problem, did he need to literally wash those bugs, *both emotional and physical,* right out of his hair?

Illustration 5. I've heard of people who couldn't wear watches because the watch would run fast, slow or periodically stop. Could the metaphysical cause for this come from the person's own feelings that time is slipping away from them? Or could it be that since everything physical and non-physical is composed of electromagnetic energy, there may simply be interference between the person's non-physical electromagnetic energy in relation to the actual watch?

Illustration 6. Over the years I have had several students tell stories about how the brakes on their car had either locked up or failed to stop and caused an accident. Interestingly enough, these "accidents" always occurred when the "victims" felt they didn't have control of their lives. I myself have had dreams/nightmares of my steering or brakes giving out during certain earlier times in my life when I didn't feel in charge of my life.

These six illustrations are a few examples based on my observations. You may be skeptical, but skepticism is extremely healthy. I only ask that you observe events in your life and the lives of those around you and decide for yourself if a connection between physical, "inanimate" objects and your emotional or mental state is possible.

ৰ্থ ৎৃ ৰ্থ ৎৃ

Let's review the important aspects of your new way of thinking, feeling, perceiving, and yes, believing. First and foremost the primary relationship is with self and its connection with the higher self, God, or whatever word you feel comfortable using. The quality and health of these relationships will determine all your other relationships because your daily life reflects those essential relationships.

Next it is important to take full self-responsibility for your interpersonal relationships. *I can't over emphasize enough that my definition of responsibility does not imply guilt or blame.* It means to grant yourself opportunities and the ability to be in charge of your own life. It encourages the increase of choices and the reduction of "shoulds", "shouldn'ts", "can'ts" and "have to's". In summary, it is not relinquishing your power to others no matter if it's a friend, relative or work associate. It is your choice whether or not you wish to hand over your emotions, your life choices and the creation of events in your life for others to manipulate. Is it your life or someone else's? It's always your choice.

Next comes your relationship with the rest of creaturehood, including mother earth. Humans vibrate with all of nature and are interconnected with the living, conscious, breathing mother earth. The feeling tones that humans emit join similar emissions from rocks, plants, trees, soil and water to co-create the weather. Natural disasters are usually created for two reasons: 1) To balance nature whether through natural evolution changes or to heal itself from the outside negative effects of man. Many times high temperatures or droughts act on the earth very much the same as our bodies do when we have a high temperature fever. The body uses a high temperature as a defense mechanism to kill off a virus. Nature may be using a drought in the same way -- possibly to kill off something that is hurting the land. Or 2) a natural disaster may be the result of collective mass consciousness where many people will change the atmosphere because of too much negativity. However, usually the outcome is beneficial because the disaster will force people to work from a point of power, co-operate and serve others, be grateful for their lives and even receive federal funding to rebuild entire communities. Once again, it's nature creating balance with its natural propensity for healing.

Finally, we need to look at our relationship with our brothers and sisters throughout the world and the universe at large. As humankind forgives and releases the old limiting institutions that brought about slavery, sexism, racism, imperialism and oppression, we can embrace multi-culturalism. The multi-cultural movement will culminate into a new race consciousness where the new human race will celebrate its similarities and place more emphasis on its common ground and less on its differences. Only then will the world truly reflect the old phrase "E Pluribus Unum" -- Latin for "Out of many, one." Then all the races and spiritual communities will end their national patriotism, hatred, prejudice and wars and will embrace all people as one universe, one people, one destiny.

Conscious Life Creations:
Work/Career

The next area we will examine is that of work/career. Although we have discussed general beliefs in the arena of money and resources earlier in the book, we will focus on this subject that is so interesting to so many people. How many people do you know who really look forward to going to work each day? Do you love your work? As I conduct one of my workshops entitled *"Discovering Your Life's Purpose and Attracting Abundance,"* I emphasize how much time you spend at work versus the amount of time you spend with your family. When you think about how much of your life and time is devoted to work, you begin to realize that you can't afford not to find a job you enjoy, one that gives you a personal sense of purpose and a compensation not solely monetary but in addition offers rewards of satisfaction, joy and fulfillment. At these workshops I ask participants their primary reason for attending and most reply with, "I want to make more money!" And when asked why, most will respond with, "I want to give my family and my- self security." Then I tell them, "But all the money and material possessions in the world will not guarantee happiness, security, health or a longer life."

Among my students I have seen those who had hundreds of thousands of dollars compare themselves to those who had millions and feel poor. And it has been my experience that even the people with millions weren't guaranteed happiness. However, I have observed the following fascinating trends and common characteristics among the wealthy, healthy and happy. Most of these individuals:

1. Discovered their life's purpose and consequently created their life's work based on their purpose.

2. Love their occupation which brings them not only financial prosperity but lots of JOY, vitality, enthusiasm and extra dividends of general well being, love and awareness.

3. Are inner directed. Each decided the type of work they wanted to do, and how to market themselves, their product or their services, being guided by their <u>own intuitions</u> instead of outside directives.

4. Exemplify self-confidence and usually exude energy and charisma.

5. Are trusting of others and the world in general, and believe in their own abilities. They are basically optimistic, expecting the most favorable outcome during any challenge.

6. They are generous, always contributing back to their community, realizing, consciously or unconsciously, that the more you give the more you will receive.

7. Surround themselves with abundance and quality. They place an emphasis on first class quality.

8. Demonstrate their love, happiness and joy in their personal, family and social life, as well as at their place of business.

9. Are extremely grateful to life and everyone in their life.

10. Have healthy self-esteems. They often have a high level of creativity, are assertive and have energy that is focused and directed.

11. Live each day with a positive mental attitude, praising others while rarely judging.

12. Feel and act as if they are worthy of the best that life has to offer, deserving of abundance and *receptive to receiving*!

Of course, this list reflects the characteristics of people I have encountered who are truly the personification of self-actualized, abundant, prosperous human beings. I'm sure you know plenty of people who may have a surplus of money in their savings along with impressive financial portfolios who seldom spend money for vacations or other pleasures and who are reluctant to share their "financial wealth" with others. They may even drive across town to purchase an item that may cost twenty cents less than at a market closer to home. Their core belief is the scarcity belief -- that there is not enough so in order to ensure future security you must hoard money. This is not prosperity because you are not free to enjoy life.

A major impediment to freedom comes when someone enters into an occupation because of parental influences or settles for a lesser job because of lack of confidence in their ability to secure or do a job that is satisfying and fulfilling and pays enough.

Most people fall into one of two categories. Either they are not self-reliant and responsible or they become the other extreme, "Mr." or "Miss" Responsible. This person usually suffers from the disease known as "OUGHTISTIC" thinking, believing they ought to please everyone, but finally coming to the conclusion that they can never please everyone, so they might as well just please themselves.

The purpose of **BELIEFOLOGY** is to encourage you to examine the beliefs that have created your reality in order to transform those beliefs that are responsible for keeping you from enjoying the life you really desire. Most people who are unhappy with their jobs or lives in general are so because they are not getting *what they want* out of their job or life. And it's probably because they *never really knew what they wanted.* Do you know what you want and what truly fulfills you? Do you know your life's purpose? What would you like to contribute to the world? Do you enjoy your job and find it fulfilling? Does your employer value your service and pay you accordingly?

Take some time to try these exercises:

1. Relax and reminisce about your last year including all the seasons. Name ten moments/events that made you feel completely fulfilled and that you really enjoyed greatly.
2. If you only had two more days to live, how would you live them?
3. If your Fairy God Mother granted you five wishes what would they be?
4. If you're older, and if you could return to age 21 and could instantly have any career, name five you would desire.
5. If you won $10 million in a lottery, describe your life style.

Now let me share my rationale for using these exercises. The first exercise is to help you realize just what makes you happy and fulfilled. Read the following responses. The first five responses are mine. I like:

1. Sitting outside on my balcony drinking ice tea and listening to the birds as I read books.
2. Listening to music.
3. Wading in the ocean.
4. Going for a ride in farm country with my life partner.
5. Walking in the woods with my life partner.

The next five responses are the most common ones I hear from my workshop participants. I like:

1. Going on a picnic with my family.
2. Playing golf.
3. Playing tennis.
4. Making love.
5. Watching T.V.

Do you see a pattern here? Many of the things people really enjoy doing have little, if anything to do with money.

After all, money itself doesn't make us happy. It's the experience, things or freedom that it provides that makes us happy!

In answer to the question, "If you only had two days left, how would you live them?" I often hear many of the same responses as number 1. However it seems as though most people would prefer to spend their time with family and their very closest friends.

Answers to the remaining questions are often intriguing. When I first started conducting workshops and individual sessions with students I thought people would choose items or experiences that would require substantial wealth or miracles in health or changes in circumstances to achieve. Believe it or not, most people selected fantasies that in my opinion they could still manifest in their lifetime! I continue to use these exercises because they help people identify what it is that makes them happy. Not only does this help lead them to their life's purpose, but it also affords them the opportunity to identify the *erroneous beliefs* that prevented them from pursuing their true career or the lifestyle that they really desire! Not only have many of us avoided our preferred profession because of interference from authorities (parents, friends, a teacher), but we've denied our success because of our own doubts, fears and limitations. *You create your life* according to your *beliefs, feelings and expectations.* Therefore *change* your *beliefs* and *you will change your life*!

When it comes to making decisions about career goals we often make excuses for ourselves. For instance, although it was and still is true that I find much of formal education as merely earning a grade instead of learning for the sake of learning, I always used this as an excuse for not continuing my formal education. But this was only partially true. After doing extensive belief work, I figured out that there was a part of me that was reluctant to further my formal education because of self-doubt and a belief that I couldn't learn math. Furthermore,

77

a severe learning disability not only affected my ability to express myself, but also exhibited itself in distractibility and other learning limitations. Nevertheless, instead of being totally honest with myself about my true beliefs about my learning disabilities, I rationalized by faulting the limitations of formal education. Since I wasn't willing to complete college in order to be successful, it was necessary for me to transform another mass belief -- that you must have a college degree to gain certain employment.

Often we limit our choices in life and merely survive instead of going for the "GUSTO" and enjoying life to the fullest with fervent passion, awareness, enthusiasm and a wonderful quest for more life! We have a tendency to rationalize and make excuses to prevent us from obtaining our desired life instead of doing belief work and taking the required actions to manifest our dreams. After you review your responses to the five questions, evaluate the beliefs that prevented you from bringing your dreams to fruition. For those careers that may not be realistic for you to achieve at this point in your life, I guarantee you that there is something in its general area that may give you comparable fulfillment. For example, if your wish was to be a ballet dancer, perhaps you could get a job with a production company doing marketing or public relations. Others who may have desired to be an artist but didn't feel artistic enough could become art collectors and start an art gallery. I had former students who put on the top of their "Fairy God Mother" list "to be financially well-off" and "to attract a marital partner". After intensive belief work some have fulfilled both wishes by attracting a wealthy partner!

Listen to your inner-self, your deepest passions, and then examine your conscious beliefs and trade the limiting ones for new, empowering beliefs. With these new convictions, develop a partnership with the powers of the universe to enjoy your new work, consistent with your newly discovered life purpose. Remember, every time you put your request out to the universe, your casting studio will attract all the actors, actresses and props to create the play according to what you think you deserve and is possible.

We are embarking upon exciting times. The next decade will bring more changes in the lives of human beings than in any other decade in the history of mankind. Change will be the rule and not the exception. Yes, change can bring great stress and anxiety, but try to focus on the myriad of opportunities that these changes will bring. Because of the collapse of our historical institutions as discussed in previous chapters, our world will see new ways of making, investing and spending money. People will realize that it is not beneficial to themselves or the world to remain in an unfulfilling job. People will discover that if they do what they love, then what they love will support them. Mother earth is in labor and will gradually deliver a new universal consciousness. Together with this new consciousness will be an acceleration and intensification of energy on our planet. Consequently your desires, beliefs and expectations will be manifested at a more rapid pace than ever before.

As I've said throughout this book, *BELIEFOLOGY* isn't original. Unfortunately though, many of the concepts in this book have been avoided by those who do not wish to become personally responsible for themselves. However, there are two major transformations referred to in this book that will bring about important changes: thought is energy and the recognition that more can be achieved for everyone by cooperating instead of competing. Mankind will recognize that the old institutions were competition based because of core beliefs of scarcity, fear and judgment. The recognition and acceptance of universal natural laws will reveal, through practical outcomes, the fact that there is no need to struggle. By following the natural laws of prosperity and targeting your purpose, you can enjoy a fulfilling job with little or no physical effort, making more money than you ever made previously with sweat, overtime and worry.

Be willing to let go of erroneous beliefs, inharmonious relationships, unfulfilling jobs and fears that no longer serve your higher good. You should acknowledge these beliefs, since you once attracted them, but now you can release them with unconditional love and replace them with powerful thoughts of confidence, trust, harmonious relationships and productive work that will not only serve your higher purpose but will contribute to the benefit of others. The advent of this new world consciousness will increase entrepreneurial opportunities and will change the world of economics as well as transform business and politics forever!

Once you've discovered your life's work and recognize your intrinsic talents and inherent skills, you will find an enhanced self-esteem, self-love and self-worth. Increase your ability to feel worthy and deserving of an occupation that will provide you with lots of money, health, joy and fulfillment.

ఆ ౨ ఆ ౨

The last item to address in this chapter is the importance of clarifying your goals and the subsequent agreement of partners and clients. Clarification intent and preferred outcome is imperative since the universe always provides us with a replica of our thoughts and expectations. In other words, "Be careful what you wish for because it can come true!"

ఆ ౨ ఆ ౨

I encourage you to discover the things and experiences that give you the greatest fulfillment, joy, happiness and peace in order for you to attract similar or even better opportunities. Next, find your life's purpose and careers that are in line with your purpose. And finally, identify beliefs and transcend those erroneous beliefs that prevented the fruition of your dreams.

Reflect back on your childhood and remember what you enjoyed and the dreams you desired. Listen to the child within for clues to rekindle those inner passions to develop new visions based on original urges. Do what you love and it will indeed take care of you, drawing to you the people, events or money to fulfill your desires. Trust and be confident, and know that there is a way to do what you love! Many times it was well-intentioned parents or teachers that limited us from dreaming our real desires. Always remember that our parents had practical reasons for wanting to protect us and that they were always doing the best they could with the beliefs they accepted. Now is the time to find out what has stopped you from doing what you want at work, as well as with your leisure time.

Examine those beliefs that claim that you are not capable. Return to the earlier chapter on Money/Resources and work in tandem with that information to enhance your prosperity. *The transformation of your scarcity and worthiness beliefs are imperative!* I remember the first class I taught on "Creating Your Reality". In two hours I made what I typically made in two days of hard work. As I drove home counting the money I made from teaching the class, I realized that what was even more exciting was that *I had so much fun* giving the class I would have paid the participants! Guess what happened? While I was driving along counting my effortlessly earned money, I looked into my rear-view mirror and saw red lights flashing behind me. You guessed it -- I got a ticket for speeding! And the fine I had to pay was exactly what I was paid for the class! I believe I created this event because at that point in my life I did not feel worthy or deserving of getting paid well for doing something that was so much fun and brought me so much inner fulfillment and peace. Obviously, I overcame that belief and I now enjoy being paid to assist others in creating a life for themselves full of health, prosperity and happiness. So you can see how deservability and worthiness beliefs influence many situations.

ENJOY YOUR NEW OPPORTUNITIES. BUT DON'T RUSH THEIR ARRIVAL. TRUST IN YOUR VISION AND ALLOW THE BEST TO FIND YOU!

Conscious Life Creations:
Judgment/Religion to Spirituality

One of the major objectives of *BELIEFOLOGY* is to encourage you to accept total responsibility for your life and to consciously create the life you truly desire. There is one issue that once overcome could bring more transformation then you could ever imagine. This issue is judgment -- the shame/ blame game that is at the root of so many of our problems, diseases, unhappiness and poverty. Before I became aware of the effects of judgment, I had no idea of its implications, nor did I realize how much in life, including our institutions, has a foundation based on judgment. I'm not talking about objective judgment such as discernment. I'm referring to value judgments consisting of "good or bad" and "right or wrong" and all the subsequent implications thereof.

Unfortunately, much of the origin of value judgment is based in the religious belief of a judgmental, personalized God and "his" much preached about "Judgment Day". Conversely, *BELIEFOLOGY* is based on the new order of thought that has been embraced by certain spiritual and science (especially quantum physics) organizations. The tenet of this philosophy is that the human mind is a part of the Universal Mind that is the origin of everything as well as the everlasting source, energy and intelligence of that greater whole. Furthermore, this conscious, awarized energy, essence or gestalt simultaneously individualizes itself through us as expressions of physical spirits.

WE ARE SPIRIT MADE FLESH!

83

The essence, purpose and motivation of this divine spiritual cosmic intelligence is unconditional love and infinite, boundless creativity!

The earth is only one of the billions of universes that are a part of this divine gestalt, and a world where all of its creaturehood is governed by universal natural law. The essence of this law for humankind is that since we are all individualized expressions of the universal mind then whatever we consciously think and mold into our consciousness will mold and manifest itself in our physical world.

LIFE IS A DO-IT-YOURSELF PROJECT!

Contrary to what you've heard before, "Life is Fair". Life supports us in whatever we put forth in consciousness. Whatever we "mind", the universe "matters". So if we place in our mind thoughts of poverty, sickness, violence and unfairness, the universe will respond with "Yes, we can do," and will replicate that thought in your daily life. However, if you place in your consciousness abundance, unconditional love/acceptance of others, health and power, then the UNIVERSE will reply with "Yes, *We Can Do*" and this will manifest in your daily reality. So as it has been proclaimed and written many times, "As Much As We Can Believe Will Be Done Unto Us." Consciousness is the cause and manifestation is the effect.

Because this larger, ALL THAT IS, God is totally accepting of all its co-creators, it intrinsically grants free will to all to create whatever they believe and desire. This God knows only good, therefore, "Good and Evil" is a man-made condition created out of ignorance and allowed to exist on earth because of free will. We experience good and evil only because man created that concept out of fear and the illusion of being separate and apart from the ALL THAT IS, universal, intelligent GOD! Reverse the letters in the word *EVIL* and see what it spells --*LIVE*. The only "evil" is when you are not being your natural GOD-Self. In other words, when you are not *LIVE-ING!* It is your own choice because there isn't an external evil force like a *D-evil*. So the opposite of *EVIL* is *LIVE!* To fully live is to embrace self, others and life with vibrant joy, power, love, exuberant energy and vitality!

The same goes for *SIN*. The origin of the word sin is an archer's term for "missing the mark." Accordingly we have a built in barometer we refer to as our conscience that will alert us if we are off life's track and need to make some adjustments in our thinking, decisions and actions that will have better consequences for all concerned. There is no God that punishes or judges us. As my friends Gordon and Amel often say *SIN* stands for "Self Inflicted Nonsense." If you consider this premise, then you realize that essentially there is no right and wrong, as well as no good and bad. Thus you have no victims, only cause and effect that results in feelings that are either beneficial/non-beneficial or favorable/unfavorable. So life is neither Good nor Bad -- life *is!* If you are feeling guilty, you will probably attract a person or event in your life to punish you. Man has created most of our institutions based on this limiting framework of reward and punishment. I cannot emphasize enough how absorbed into our consciousness, both individual and collectively, is this fear driven "Good-Bad" framework. From this framework comes JUDGMENT.

Let's explore the concept of judgment and it's practical implications. Judgment is the product of the aforementioned Good/Bad, Right/Wrong framework and comes out of fear and produces guilt.

> ***WHEN YOU JUDGE YOU CREATE***
> ***A BONDAGE BETWEEN YOU***
> ***AND WHAT IT IS YOU'RE JUDGING.***

Consequently, this negative emotion establishes an attachment to whatever is being judged and will breed more judgment.

How many people do you know who suffer from the shame/ blame game? Judgment perpetuates this endless cycle that *keeps us stuck to what it is we are blaming*. Taking responsibility and living from a point of power frees us! Blame is caused by a loss of personal identity with your God-Self. Otherwise you would have no need to judge because you will be too busy living your own life. Instead of placing “shoulds” or “shouldn'ts” on yourself or others, replace the “shoulds” with “coulds”. “Could” denotes free choice, whereas judgments and “should” imply "Right or Wrong" and "Good and Bad."

Here’s an analogy I like to use to demonstrate this concept. Say you’re driving down the highway and you’re daydreaming and you miss your exit. Now your immediate need is to start concentrating and choose the "best" detour that will enable you to return to your chosen direction. To get angry and berate yourself may distract you more and possibly make you lose your focus, taking you further from your path. Isn’t this what we often do in our daily lives when we miss our goals or purpose? Instead of merely redirecting ourselves, we attract retaliation from others that places us further from our fulfillment or leads us further from our chosen path. Or if we are not blaming ourselves for our mistakes we may try to find someone else to blame, even for trivial things like tripping, falling or breaking something. This is just as self-destructive.

There are many ways we attract judgments and punishments. Most accidents are caused by one of the following reasons:

1. We are not concentrating on what we are doing, in other words, not being “in the now”;

2. Our life is out of balance and we draw in an accident to re-balance ourselves, often putting our priorities in place;

3. Similar to number 2, but more specifically, life is telling us to slow down. Often traffic tickets are a sign from the universe suggesting the need to slow our lives down, to "find balance"; and

4. Finally, and the reason most relevant to our inner-self, is that accidents are caused by the belief in the need for punishment.

These kinds of accidents can manifest themselves from insignificant, small incidents to serious accidents that result in critical injuries and substantial financial cost. If you cut your finger while peeling vegetables it may be because of carelessness. But if you shut the same finger in the car door and the next day you get the same hand bit by a dog, chances are you're feeling guilty about something and you're punishing yourself.

GUILT SEEKS OUT PUNISHMENT!

Often it occurs in multiple events. Take the husband who decided he couldn't tolerate his unreasonable boss any longer and quit his job without securing future employment. This father had a strong belief that it is the total responsibility of the man to be the sole breadwinner. But the mother of his two children was forced to work. Since the mother had never worked, the family only had one car. So the husband had to take his wife to work everyday before pursing employment interviews.

One day while transporting his wife to work, their car was demolished when another car hit them after running a stop sign. The other driver didn't have any insurance. Neither did the man and his wife. They had allowed the car insurance to lapse

87

because of their financial condition. So the wife had to quit her job because they had no transportation.

Right when this family thought things couldn't get any worse, the husband fell off the porch and broke his right foot! Now many people may be convinced that this man was just a victim of bad luck. But **BELIEFOLOGY** stresses that there are no accidents or victims. Could it be that this man drew in his accidents because of his beliefs about his role as a breadwinner? Did he break his right foot because of his fear of not "getting off on the right foot" with a new boss? Or because he didn't feel good about how he was standing in life? Are these theories far fetched? Please be skeptical, but observe the people in your life and you will begin to view events as a mirror of their thoughts, feelings and belief patterns. This demonstrates the theme that runs throughout this book -- *as the inner, so the outer!*

꧁ ꧂ ꧁ ꧂

I think one of my best lessons on judgment came when I was judging the federal government. It was in the early eighties and I was staying in a hotel in Florida for several weeks to plant the seeds to launch my new business in that state. I spent a lot of my spare time watching public TV in my hotel room. I really became intensely involved in a television series on Vietnam that aired for several days straight. My attention focused on the American atrocities and the hundreds of dead soldiers and the families back home that were left in confusion because of our federal government's involvement in this war.

To make matters worse, I also watched a broadcast with a comment from the current President, referring to Russians as being a part of an evil empire. In the same broadcast were excerpts from the President echoing the mass belief that capitalism is good and America has God on its side while communism is not only wrong but evil. He reminded Americans of the cold war and the erroneous collective belief that communism must be destroyed at any cost! It's no wonder I was concentrating on the "bad", authoritarian aspects of the establishment instead of focusing on all the positive characteristics of the federal government. I sat down and wrote a letter to my partner, Leslie, who had stayed back in Ohio, and told her that I needed to get out of my room because I was spending too much time watching television and I was becoming too negative. I went to the post office to mail my letter and as I was parking my car I noticed a policeman abusing a senior citizen parked nearby.

I approached the policeman and asked, "What's going on here, what did he do?"

The officer responded, "Either you leave or I will arrest you!"

I said, "Before I go, just what is your name?" At that point the officer grabbed my arm and handcuffed me.

I said, "This isn't necessary and by the way you're hurting my arm."

Suddenly, a man ran out from the post office, pulled a gun on me and asked the policeman if he needed any assistance. It turned out that this man was an FBI agent who was at the post office on official business. The policeman assured the FBI agent that he had everything under control, that he was taking me to the police station for interfering with an arrest and resisting arrest.

Riding in the police car, I stabilized my emotions and it finally occurred to me what was happening. Because I was concentrating lately on the "injustice" system and the federal government, I drew in the proof of my belief that authority figures can be unfair and at times cruel and heartless. I have stated it many times before in this book, and it was true for me in this situation: You get what you concentrate on and your life's daily events and experiences will always reinforce and "prove your beliefs." Because, I was concentrating on Vietnam and judging the federal government I drew in a judgment drama at a federal building with an FBI agent and a policeman who symbolized authority figures. The elderly man reflected my belief in how seniors and the disabled are neglected and at times abused. As I realized why I drew this event in, I became less judgmental and the policeman's personality altered and he became more personable and friendly. As we left the police car and I was escorted to the holding cell, the policeman explained to me this version of what happened. The policeman told me that the old man refused to sign a paper acknowledging his receipt of a ticket, punctuating his refusal with a profanity. The policeman felt the need to teach the man some respect. He believed that "old people" were getting as bad as young people about not respecting authority.

Later, the senior citizen contacted me. He explained that his wife had just had a mastectomy and because he was so distracted, he probably had violated a traffic law. The police officer was trying to get the man to sign the ticket just as an acknowledgment of the receipt of the citation. But the elderly gentleman thought it was an admission of guilt. And he admitted cursing at the policeman. Later at his court hearing, the senior citizen was allowed to tell his side of the story and all the extra charges were dropped. I thought about pursuing charges of police brutality, but then I remembered that it was my judging that brought about my role in this drama and by pressing charges against the policeman I would only attract further events in the blame/ shame game.

I learned my lesson about judgment. So many people in today's culture thrive on judgment, revenge and manipulation. Critics blame television and Hollywood for the violence in America. I believe these shows are produced and are profitable because they are a reflection and therefore appeal to the mass collective belief system. Notice that the so-called "family" shows aren't as popular or in demand as the action-packed, violence and sex-filled productions. Many life-affirming television shows have been replaced by TV series that focus on deceit, revenge, violence, vindication, jealousy and possessiveness.

Judgment is a product of fear and beliefs perpetrated by religions and science. We have come to believe that our very nature is flawed and weak and, according to certain religions, that we are born with sin and are guilty until proven innocent. Therefore man created government and laws to protect people from people, and from life. We see chaos, crime, murder and drug problems around us and we think we need to establish more laws and rules. But many of these problems are caused by the entire framework (judgment) of good and bad that creates the need for rigid regulations.

The new power/peace paradigm recognizes that you cannot fight for peace, rather you have to live and be peaceful. This is why the war on drugs and the war on poverty are futile. War is based on judgment and many times judgment leads to guilt and hate. Moreover hate and guilt are great energizers that culminate in massive destruction. This cycle can be broken when we cease judging and allow each person the right to be different. As you grant yourself the freedom to be yourself so shall you allow others the freedom to be themselves. I'm not saying that you need to spend your energy and time hanging out with people you don't feel comfortable with. Become life affirming and flow with your natural preferences and propensities in a loving, peaceful direction according to your inner guidance. Refuse to give up your power and peace to those who may attempt to bring you down to their limiting, judgmental belief system. When you enter the judgment zone you are no longer proactive but a reactive victim.

Instead, become more self-directed. Outer recognition and reinforcements motivate you to be dependent on outer influences. Don't give up your real desires, fulfillment and power in order to seek out outer validation, or make decisions based on fear of punishment instead of healthy choices motivated by what's beneficial for all concerned. And don't judge yourself for not always creating a reality of your preference. So many people, when they initially accept the responsibility of creator-ship, may be hard on themselves whenever they draw unfavorable experiences into their lives. Remember that you are in the process of unlearning all the erroneous beliefs you've blindly accepted all these years. Gradually you will release old patterns that have created artificial fences so you can fly free and enjoy a healthy, happy life. Forgive yourself, love yourself, accept yourself, allow yourself, embrace yourself and express your divine powerful self and your new beneficial beliefs will manifest themselves more and more.

SPIRITUALITY

Now let's review the major shift in consciousness that is causing paradigm transitions and creating inner realizations and a natural propensity toward natural living and everlasting freedom! This shift includes the awakening of each human being with the enlightenment and realization that we are all sons and daughters of God, learning how to consciously create a harmonious reality.

This author believes that there was a man named Jesus who was endowed with the Christ consciousness and developed more of his potential than any other human being. However, I feel that every human being is just as divine. It would be beneficial to let go of the picture of Jesus on the cross and create your own personal Easter by being your own savior and end your own suffering by taking responsibility for your own reality.

Likewise, I believe other teachers like Buddha, Confucius and Mohammed were also enlightened souls who helped many people. I believe it's beneficial for us to study and accept that part of Judaism, Christianity, Islam, Hinduism, Taoism,

Buddhism, as well as beliefs of our Native Americans, that are life affirming and connect intuitively with what we personally feel spiritually. I consider myself an extremely spiritual person, but hardly a religious person. The book the "Prophet" by Khalil Gibran probably expresses my spiritual feelings and beliefs more than any religion. As we enter a new millennium, I think the only chance for the survival of any religion is if they accept that there is no separation between the Father-Mother-God and Human beings, and they eliminate the rigid paternal dogma that binds the masses to a religion. It's time to stop following blindly what generations of people have not dared to question and to listen within to your own inner authority. A former student and good friend of mine, Marty Segal, expressed this well when he chose as the title of his book *The Guru is You*.

Unfortunately, many people interpret Western and Eastern religions and philosophy to mean that in order to be spiritual you must renounce worldly things like money and material possessions. Furthermore, they encouraged people to deny sexuality and all ego desires. Although I think we are happier when we are not attached to things or relationships, I don't think we would have a physical body, physical things or an ego if we weren't meant to enjoy them. Instead of transcending your human nature and denying your sexuality and ego, accept and enjoy these natural expressions. Of course, in order to live happy, harmonious, productive and fulfilling lives we also need to balance and moderate all of these natural aspects.

It is unhealthy to repress or suppress energy because energy has to express itself. You can see for yourselves how in a society where religious and other institutions have discouraged sex how popular sex is and how it sells. Psychology and religions, including new age thought and the self-improvement movements perpetuate judgment by perceiving the ego as an enemy that must be eradicated. We could not live in a physical universe without the ego because it's the navigator of our lives. It's only when the ego is out of balance with the other aspects of our personality and spiritual essence that it becomes a negative force. Embrace the wonderment, beauty, feelings, power, pleasure and joy of your physical bodies. Although you are more than your physical selves, it is still your temporary vehicle and should be cherished and enjoyed.

I believe that the hope, as well as the solutions to most of society's problems is spiritual in nature. Historically, man has projected many of his limiting, neurotic and sometimes even psychotic-personalities onto this deity. Humans have developed institutions that reflected the characteristics of a jealous God who demands conditional respect and obedience and for all to worship and fear. Man has created God in his limiting image, instead of realizing that God is so much more omnipotent, powerful, beautiful, awesome, prosperous and indefinable than most humans can comprehend.

By releasing the old institutions and the old erroneous mass beliefs, we will witness the merging of science, religion and medicine. Men and women will reclaim their power and realize that even though there is always a power greater than ourselves we are a connected part of that universal intelligence and that as we each evolve in consciousness we can tap into more and more of that infinite and eternal source. As we become more *involved* in consciously creating our reality, we will become more *evolved.*

❧ ❧ ❧ ❧

In my studies of theology and a number of religions, I have noticed a common theme running throughout -- love, faith and trust. I challenge any Christian to explore the teachings of Jesus, as well as certain parts of the old testament, because if you examine them objectively you will see many of the concepts in **BELIEFOLOGY** are right there in the bible.

Remember the Bible and other religious works were written by man many centuries ago based on the collective beliefs of that era. In addition, many of the translated words no longer have the same meanings. The Bible is actually one of the most misinterpreted books. I also believe much of the Bible was tampered with by certain political and religious factions in order to control and manipulate their followers. In fact, I believe that there were entire chapters eliminated. The interpretation I believe of "heaven" is a state of wholeness and happiness -- in other words, in harmony with our God-self. I do not believe that there is an entity or being that is a devil no more than I believe there is a place called HELL. Nevertheless, I do interpret the biblical word hell as a mental and emotional condition or state of being that has as its experiences disease and discordance. Hell is the opposite of my metaphysical definition of heaven. Like heaven, the word kingdom is an inner state of being (the kingdom of heaven is within). Evil, like devil, is any thing or experience that seems destructive and separates itself from our God-self. And SIN is a term for "missing the mark." It is merely a demonstration of the law of cause and effect. When a person makes a mistake there is a consequence. There is not an outside God or Devil punishing us for our "sins" (mistakes). There is a natural consequence. We must realize that we are a dynamic part of an infinite power and everlasting love.

Take some time to reflect on these quotes from the Judeo-Christian Bible and various other religious books:

Is it not written in your law, I have said you are Gods. (John 10:34)

Ask and it shall be given you, seek and ye shall find; knock and it shall be opened to you. (Matt. 7:7)

On that day you will know that I am in my father and you in me and I in you. (John 14:20)

95

If you have faith as small as a mustard seed, you can say to this mountain, move from here to there and it will move. Nothing will be impossible for you. (Matthew 17:20)

All things are possible to him that believeth. (Mark 9:23)

The Kingdom of God is within you. (Luke 17:20)

Be ye transformed by the renewing of your mind. (Romans 12:2)

As thou has believed, so be it done unto thee. (Matt 8:13)

Judge not, that ye be not judged. (Matt 7:1)

Things which are seen were not made of things which do appear. (Heb 11:3)

All things whatsoever ye pray and ask for, believe that ye received them, and ye shall have them. (Mark 11:22-24)

Freely have ye received, freely give. (Matthew 10:8)

In him we live, and move, and have our being. (Acts 17:28)

Let not your heart be troubled, neither let it be fearful. (John 14:27)

That is perfect, this is perfect, perfect comes from perfect. Take perfect from perfect, the remainder is perfect. (The Upanishads)

Not God but ye yourselves are the creators and supporters of moral evils. (The Talmud)

It's your Father's good pleasure to give you the kingdom. (Luke 12:32)

And you shall know the truth, and the truth shall make you free." (John 8:32)

Be still and know that I am God. (Psalm 46:10)

The ordinary person's mind is the same as the sages, because the original mind is perfect and complete in itself. (Pai-Chang)

If you bring forth what is inside you, what you bring forth will save you. (The Gospel of Thomas)

Be in a realm where neither good nor evil exists. . . in the presence of unity there is neither command nor prohibition. (Aba Yazid Al-Bistami)

And where do name and form both cease, and turn to utter nothingness? And the answer is, 'in consciousness invisible and infinite, of radiance bright. (Buddhism)

The Atman (the real self) is permanent, eternal and therefore existence itself. (Hindu Philosophy)

It (God) was not created in the past, nor is it to be annihilated in the future; it is eternal, permanent, absolute; and for all eternity it sufficiently embraces in its essence all possible merits. (Buddhism)

All that is with you passeth away, but that which is with God abideth. (The Koran)

Realize that there are 'that' (Brahman) "which is the cessation of all differentiation's, which never changes to nature and is as unnerved as a waveless ocean, eternally unconditioned and undivided. (Hindu Philosophy)

By knowledge of God (Deva) all the bonds (of ignorance, unhappiness, etc.) are destroyed. (Upanishad)

To everything there is a season, and a time to every purpose under heaven. (Ecclesiates 3:1)

The stranger who resides with you shall be to you as one born among you, and you shall love him as yourself. (Leviticus 19:34)

Thou openest thy hand, and satisfies the desire of every living thing. (Psalm 145:16)

Understanding is a wellspring of life unto him that hath it. (Proverbs 16:22)

And behold, I am with thee, and will keep thee in all places whether thou goest. (Genesis 28:15)

There is that scattereth, and yet increaseth. (Proverbs 11:24)

Theirs was the fullness of heaven and earth; the more that they gave to others, the more they had. (TAOISM)

He who is happy within, who rejoiceth within, who is illuminated within becoming the Eternal, goeth to the Peace of the Eternal. (The Bhagavad Gita)

You are the light of the world. (Matthew 5:14)

Blessed are the peacemakers: for they shall be called the children of God. (Matthew 5:9)

Bless are the merciful: for they shall obtain mercy. (Matthew 5:7)

God is love. (I John 4:8)

Blessed are the meek (flexible): for they shall inherit the earth. (Matthew 5:5)

He that is of a merry heart hath a continual feast. (Proverbs 15:15)

ↄ৯ ৯৯ ↄ৯ ৯৯

"We are not physical beings having a spiritual experience, but spiritual beings having a physical experience." In other words, we are not enclosed in our bodies. Tap into your powerful self and you will leave religious dogma in the past and become the spiritual being you were designed to be, every moment of your daily life.

5 BEYOND BELIEFS TO KNOWING

Inner-Directed Living & Empowering the Moment

Once you have eliminated your erroneous and limiting beliefs, you will want to move to the next developmental stage of raising your consciousness. Although there may be more advanced levels possible to achieve on the earth plane, usually this is the final state of consciousness one can experience. The enhanced consciousness I'm referring to is going beyond beliefs to a life of *KNOWING*. This means being guided intuitively and *living* in the here and now.

One of my spiritual teachers, Amel, is not too keen on the word *belief* for he states, "The word belief is a phrase that says I 'be-lie', 'I have a lie' and 'I be that lie that I have.'" Although humans today are participating in an enlightening, consciousness raising evolution, as long as there are those people who "be-lie", then ignorant and erroneous "beliefs" will need to be examined. As we become and live our true/natural selves we will outlive the need for beliefs, whether or not they are favorable or unfavorable, beneficial or non-beneficial.

In this new millennium, people will be awakened with a fervent inner desire to become liberated and to enjoy this new found freedom through inner-directed living and empowering the moment. Human beings will take complete responsibility for their lives and will discover their life's purpose, thus

99

gravitating towards jobs that are fun, enjoyable and productive. You can enjoy this freedom and build upon this liberation utilizing your unlimited source *within*. It brings *everything* into your life. Accept that consciousness literally matters! Paramount to this success is the ability to trust the answers that can be discovered from within and to realize that your inner voice can reveal to your conscious self who you really are. You will no longer require beliefs about yourself or your universe because you will acquire a sense of self-knowing and will use your natural power to consciously co-create the life of choice. Your intuition is your hot line to "God", so reclaim your power and consciously reconnect with your infinite nature. Instead of going outside of yourself in prayer to something or someone out there, relax, calm and center yourself in peace and turn inward to your still, small voice inside and wait for it's guidance and direction. We often forget in this age of information and sophisticated computers that we are equipped with a bio-computer (the mind) that works in accordance with our choices. Outside computers aren't clear about our desires let alone what is going on with our body, intellect or emotions. You're born with this bio-computer that is more advanced then any computer humans will ever create. Your bio-computer working in partnership with your inner-self (and it's intuitive guidance center) is awesome.

Once you can outgrow the notion that you are somewhere outside of God and you begin to feel it, *KNOW* it, and most important *LIVE* it, you will no longer need beliefs or **BELIEFOLOGY**. You will be inner-directed and will trust yourself and the world at large. Once you accept this "knowing" of universal laws and universal "truth", you will have no excuses to hang on to your old beliefs of victimhood. Remember, responsibility does not mean "guilt," "wrong" or "bad". It means you have the choice and power to be proactive in creating your life of choice. You will know whether or not your choices are beneficial by the results you see in your daily life. Beneficial choices will bring opportunities and freedom. If you're like me, freedom will empower you.

One of the challenges you will face once you've eliminated limiting beliefs is that you will attract more opportunities than ever. Due to time constraints you may have "approach-approach" conflicts, so you may have to pick from several possibilities. This is when it is imperative to utilize your intuition and learn to choose the opportunity that is the most timely and appropriate. When you are inner-directed, your inner confidence will counteract any momentary panic caused by outer events and will prevent you from pushing events or the need to control. Remember, fear motivates us to force events. Allow me to illustrate this concept with an example from an experience of a former student.

Mary worked at an international corporation for ten years and for the last three years worked closely with the director of her department. The director encouraged this collaboration because she felt that she was grooming Mary for her job. When the director left, Mary was extremely confident that she would naturally get the director's job. Unfortunately, she didn't get the job. The corporate office sent a replacement and Mary was devastated. Mary felt that she had wasted the last three years of her career and decided to look for another job with another company. Three months later a comparable position to the one she was passed over for opened up at another company. During one of her individual sessions, Mary told me she was applying for this new position even though her intuition was telling her she should wait until something else came along. When I suggested that she follow her inner impulse, she told me that she wasn't sure if it was her intuition or just her fear because she had failed at her previous attempt at a promotion. She went to the interview but was really confounded when she didn't get the job. During her next individual session, we reviewed the reasons why she may not have gotten the job:

    A.   Initially her little voice warned her that this wasn't

her job.

B. Her consciousness may have been too different from the consciousness of the company where she was applying for a job. (No applicant can be hired into a company whose consciousness isn't comparable. Each organization has a consciousness of it's own.)

C. Perhaps her inner-self in collaboration with the universe had a better job waiting for her in the future.

For the next month, Mary was deeply depressed. Then her new director informed her of a position available in California with a competitive agency. Mary couldn't believe it. Ever since she was a child she longed to live in California. She felt very good about her chances. Not only did she get the job, but the pay was significantly higher, she felt more comfortable with her new work peers, and she got to move to an area with a more favorable climate. In retrospect she understood why she didn't get the first two jobs. If she was offered the original job, she would never have met the new director who "just happened" to have a friend working at the California company. And if she had been offered the second job, she wouldn't have been available for the "preferred" job.

The more you work with **BELIEFOLOGY** concepts, the more you will become fascinated with the synchronicity of event-making. The more you realize that your daily experiences are created from the inside out, the more conscious you will become of the benefits of inner-directed living. Begin to trust your inner-knowing and act upon your inner guidance system. While it may communicate softly, it can still relay intense feelings of love and positive intent. Impulses were the driving force for most inventors and creative minds like Edison, Ford and Einstein. You too can tap into this inner well of creative inspiration not only for ideas but for strength, confidence and support.

Other influences in our lives include behavior modification based on reward. Reward systems can be just as limiting as punishment systems because they tend to lead you away from inner-directed living. Many people will make choices and respond according to someone else's preferences and will allow people or forces outside themselves to control and have power over self. You relinquish your own inner fulfillment in pursuit of outer rewards or validation. Outer rewards will lose importance when you realize that all real fulfillment, happiness and peace come from within. Once you live your life from a position of inner security you will no longer need outward validation and approval for you will recognize that your *outer* safety springs from your real, *inner* reality. This inner energy will radiate out into your mental, emotional and physical being, embracing the vitality of the divine, powerful you! As people become more inner-directed, the human psyche will trigger unused parts of the mind, and help to develop inner technology similar to the Internet and the cyberspace network.

Gradually as we evolve consciously using this newly discovered inner hardware, humans will evolve to the level of replacing our computers with our bio-computers and we will be surfing our INNERNET instead. This new BIO/MIND technology will include going into the sleep-dream state consciously, or in our regular awake state go into a conscious trance and enter the UNIVERSAL INNERNET! Furthermore, we will become more psychic and telepathic, and instead of faxing information we will relay it telepathically and receive it through automatic writing or on our mental screen. Until this future evolution takes place we will have to rely on the tandem use of our conscious mind and our intuition. Although it's beneficial to use our intuition as our primary barometer, it's useful to use our ego and conscious mind to assess our experiences and events to know what choices and decisions to make that will manifest our intent. Often it's those chance meetings with that contact person that develops into a business, friendship or intimate relationship. You would not believe how many opportunities we miss by not following our hunches or unraveling the mystery in some of these chance encounters by exploring the adventures those opportunities can provide.

◈ ◈ ◈ ◈

In the last part of this chapter we will be discussing the importance and meaning of *Empowering the Moment*. Take a moment and think and feel about how much time you reminisce about the past, dream about the future and therefore miss the current moment. Even more limiting are those people who are stuck in the past (sometimes distant) by bitter resentments and those who are fearful and doubtful about their future. Perhaps even if the latter group could concentrate momentarily on the current moment, they would most likely bring into the moment chaos and anxiety.

Some years ago, I was reflecting on my life and I realized how much of my life I had literally wasted. Until that moment I never realized how much of my time was spent on planning the future, as well as worrying. In addition, it dawned on me that most of my life I had wasted not only time, but also energy and peace of mind on worrying about other people. This concern was especially expressed and spent on loved ones that couldn't ever understand how to change their beliefs and create a better reality for themselves. For the next year, I noticed this preoccupation and pattern of living in the future instead of enjoying the now. Even on vacation I would spend much of the time creating ideas in my mind on how I could raise money for more and better vacations. So little of my vacation time went for truly relaxing and enjoying each and every moment. Since then I've come a long way in cherishing and enjoying living in the moment. Although I've made progress, I still have a tendency to plan too much and I am often obsessed with the feeling (possible belief??) that there is never enough TIME! My greatest progress has been in the area of worrying about loved ones. I now accept the possibility that some of my loved ones will always continue their suffering, illness and other manifestations of unhappiness. However, I can love and accept them unconditionally without leaving my reality of abundance, health, happiness and peace of mind. This may be the next most difficult step in raising your consciousness after you have completed your belief work in this journey of *BELIEFOLOGY*. Although you love your friends, work mates and family, giving up your power and peace by taking on their struggles and suffering will not help them, yourself or the world.

More important to this discussion is that this concern for others will take you away from living in the moment. I'm not saying it's not okay to reminisce or dream. If there wasn't a purpose for both we wouldn't have the ability to do so, and we would act more instinctively, like the animal kingdom. Although I may have wasted some of my life by not living "in the now," I can recall the experiences that most held my attention and consumed every fiber of my being: Feelings of comfort and security when I was being held or carried as a child; experiencing the ecstasy of a thunderstorm or winter wonderland during a snow storm; enjoying beautiful music; making love and being so connected with the merging of another that all time stops with no mental or physical distraction; the fulfillment of tasting and savoring a favorite meal; the companionship of a friend or significant other while walking though the woods; remembering my father's greetings; fond memories of my mother; and saying my final good-bye to my sister as I hugged my niece, Paula. It is obvious that I must have spent some of my life living and enjoying the moment.

Life is meant to be a process, joy-filled with fascination and excitement, a mystery-filled journey. Experience and relish the totality of the moment and really, truly LIVE! By empowering the moment, and living a full, inner-directed life, regardless of what external events are going on, you will arrive at each tomorrow experiencing life to the maximum. Where you focus your "now" moment will affect how you recall your past and will determine the outcome of your future. If you hate or resent yesterday and worry about tomorrow you will most likely attract an unfavorable today.

Feel the power of love and allow more of you to be present and enjoy your experiences and become one with your creation. Enjoy and spend quality time with your parents, children, friends and significant others, because after each moment they will no longer be the same person and neither will you. Embrace and enjoy the moments you share now because there is a good-bye to every relationship and even if you believe in an after life or reincarnation neither you nor your loved ones will be the same people you are in this now moment. Enjoy and learn from your past experiences but don't dwell in the past or on the future. Plant seeds for your future and then return and bless the now and be grateful that you have given yourself the opportunity to be who and what you are, accepting yourself unconditionally. Learn to empower the moment by embracing the strength and gentleness of life and learning to be still and discover the balance, the peace, the tranquility and the quiet that is always to be found from within.

By empowering the moment, you will grow and expand and will be so fascinated with the mystery and wonderment of the journey that the past and the future will lose its hold. As several of my spiritual teachers have said, "The point of power is in the present moment and the point of *POWER* is the point of *PEACE*." Give yourself permission to embrace and enjoy yourself in this and every future moment.

6 YOUR UNIVERSE CAN BE SAFE

Now that you have become a practicing *Beliefologist*, it's time to create a healthy, prosperous, happy, wonder-filled and fulfilling life. When you successfully develop a consciousness composed of the characteristics described throughout this book, you will naturally co-create a safe living environment. Others may say to you, "But you're kidding yourself. Be realistic. Just look at our communities and you'll see proof of the unemployment, violence, disease, crime, poverty and child abuse, not to mention the information the media reports about international wars, famine and atrocious acts."

Of course the world is not safe for everyone everywhere in the world. *BELIEFOLOGY* is saying that you can create your universe within the larger cosmos and be as safe as you believe or know you can be. In spite of all the poverty, disease, crime and unfairness in the world, you will find just as many people that have never experienced these unnatural affects of powerlessness. Once more, let's explore the literal meaning of the idea that "you create your reality," an idea that is gaining so much acceptance among so many psychologists, philosopher's, physicists, medical practices, spiritual leaders and business visionaries. More and more people are coming to believe that there are no victims or accidents, and there is a reason for what appears to be a coincidence.

Example 1: Leslie and I lived in an apartment complex in the Ft. Lauderdale area and over a two-year period we probably locked our apartment at the most maybe ten times. Our next-door neighbors not only always locked their apartment, but they placed a dead bolt lock on the door for "extra" security. Within a six-month period, our next door neighbors had their door forced opened and had valuables stolen twice. We never had any trouble.

Now I don't recommend not locking your doors. With our present day fears and constant barrage of negative messages from friends and the media, it's best that you do lock your doors. I lock my home and car whenever I feel my life is out of balance or whenever my intuition suggests it's to my advantage to do so. But locks and security systems alone can't keep burglars from breaking in because there is always a "professional" who can figure out how to get around any lock or security system. However, it's the *belief* that is important, because if you feel secure with a certain lock or security system you will not send out the fear vibrations necessary to attract the criminal.

REMEMBER, YOU GET WHAT YOU CONCENTRATE ON -- FEAR ATTRACTS THE VERY THING IT FEARS.

Example 2: If you believe that certain minority groups or individuals of lower social economic levels are inferior and if you have a belief or fear that among these people are those who will hurt, rob, and in some cases may even kill you, then you may become a "victim" to these "perpetrators." The group of "perpetrators" often shares the common belief that they are the "victims" of society and that they are powerless to change the circumstances they find themselves in. Thus they often feel angry towards certain social groups and persons within that stereotypical class. Therefore, those perpetrators will rationalize any crime and feel that robbery or assault is justified because either society owes them or it's fair vengeance. Because there are no accidents or victims, in order for the "perpetrators" and the "victims" to electromagnetically draw each other into a drama, both must have similar belief systems. The primary principle in *BELIEFOLOGY* is that like consciousness attracts people, events, experiences and emotions of equivalent consciousness. One way to transform your consciousness is to change your beliefs.

CHANGE YOUR BELIEFS
AND YOU CAN CHANGE YOUR LIFE.

Example 3: I was waiting for an employee at a restaurant for a business lunch and I received a call from my office to inform me that my business guest would be late because she had an accident. When she arrived she told me about the accident, including the disappointing fact that the car was brand new. My first question was, "Don't you think you deserve a new car?" To my surprise her response was timely and appropriate for the very chapter I was working on in this book -- in fact the very paragraph! She thought for a minute and then responded to my question, "Ken, that's exactly what happened, because the only other time I had an accident was when I bought my first Chevy Cavalier and I wrecked it by running into a deer!"

She went on to explain how she and her husband debated about who "deserved" a new car. She told me that after she purchased the car she felt guilty for not letting her husband get the brand new Camaro he wanted because, after all, he really deserved it because he works so hard. This tipped me off that there might have been three factors that caused this accident. First she didn't feel she deserved the new car. Second, she was remembering what happened the last time she got a brand new car. And third, she was feeling guilty for not allowing her husband to get the new car. In a previous chapter we talked about the tendency toward self-punishment or the attraction of outside punishment or retribution whenever we feel guilty. Well, I'm sure if I could research the background events that

109

transpired in the life of the person that she hit, there would be reasons that person drew in the accident also. And on top of the accident, this woman received a traffic ticket for causing the accident, further "punishing" herself because of the "guilt."

REFLECT BACK ON ACCIDENTS OR EVENTS YOU MAY HAVE CO-CREATED TO DETERMINE IF UNRESOLVED ISSUES OF DESERVABILITY OR GUILT WERE INVOLVED.

Example 4: At the time I started exploring the concept of ***BELIEFOLOGY,*** I knew a couple that were in the process of getting a mutually decided upon, amicable divorce. During this time, their home was broken into, and although there was cash and other valuables in the house only an antique item was stolen. One spouse had inherited this antique from a grandmother, but the other spouse appreciated and enjoyed this piece of furniture more than the true owner. Each partner insisted that the other should take the precious antique and felt the other "deserved" it more. So what happened? They attracted a robber who felt *he* deserved it more than the owners. The antique item was stolen and never recovered!

∞ ∞ ∞ ∞

BELIEFOLOGY is a <u>Do-It-Yourself</u> mission to help you discover how you co-create your daily life. Observe the people in your life. Listen to the stories in the news. Do your own research. You would be surprised at the number of people who "just happened" to miss the plane that crashed that were later killed in another type of accident. And there are those people who *unconsciously* chose to miss their doomed flight who live to tell the stories of how a flat tire or an "accident" on the way to the airport made them miss the plane. If you could investigate some of the "victims" in a plane crash, you might find that some of these people felt powerless and unhappy in their lives and may have unconsciously chosen to go out of this life with a bang. Reputable universities have released research studies that found a high percentage of people who died of cancer suffered a tragic loss or had experienced an emotionally disastrous event. You may say that according to the philosophy of *BELIEFOLOGY* that all death is a suicide. But your life can be safe, healthy, prosperous and happy because that is the true nature of the universe. As you work with your beliefs and the other concepts discussed in this book, you will realize that *safety is a fact of existence.* Living from a position of faith and inner trust of the knowledge of safety, you will be safe regardless of any contradictory evidence that outside physical events may offer. Once you have reached this awareness and state of consciousness, you can walk in the most dangerous neighborhoods, or survive in the front of any battlefield and remain safe and untouched. Why do you think there are those survivors of some of the bloodiest battles in our major wars? And how about the "hero" who rescues people from a flaming inferno?

It could benefit humankind immensely if we studied healthy, happy and safe people as much or more than we study diseased, impoverished or unhappy people. Throughout the book I have suggested that you observe those around you with erroneous beliefs. In addition, observe those people in your world who live a full, healthy, prosperous and joyful life. These are the men and women who can teach you so much. Don't judge those people who may be acting out of limited consciousness because they are most likely doing the best they know how. Hopefully they will eventually attract teachers and books that will assist them in raising their consciousness. But although teachers can facilitate learning, only you can change your consciousness.

LIFE IS A DO-IT-YOURSELF PROJECT!

Never compare your progress with others. We come from a variety of backgrounds, and some of us need to *un-learn* more beliefs than others. You may find that you may make Herculean progress in one area of your life -- say for instance financial -- while you may continue to have further belief work to do in other areas like health and vitality.

Your growth and your safety are determined only by what is going on inside your heart and head. Just as no one can hurt you emotionally unless you relinquish your power and grant them the power to hurt you, it's the same with physical safety. We have been taught that we must always be on the defensive, on guard against outer influences and circumstances that can and will harm us. The new awareness is that we live in a wonder-filled, power-filled, prosperous universe that is always supporting our choices. *Life is a smorgasbord of choices that offers an entire array of experiences and it's up to us to select whatever it requires to satisfy our desires.* Life is as safe as we believe it is and it is as safe as we want to create it.

Whenever I think about issues regarding safety, security or comfort, I recall a picture one of my spiritual teachers, Carin Waddell, shared with her students. It was a picture of a cat lying very peacefully on an extremely big pillow-cushioned bed taking a nap. Under the picture she had written, "Rest in the ease and comfort of your own being." Instead of searching for something outside your "self" or controlling and shielding yourself with defensive postures, go to the power within with the eternal confidence that you do live in a safe and loving universe. The following are Louise Hay's affirmations that are very relevant and appropriate to this chapter:

Everything I need comes to me
in the perfect time, space sequence.

Under this affirmation she wrote, "I release the struggle of trying to make things happen."

Life is a joy and filled with love.

Under this affirmation she wrote, "As I choose to believe this, it becomes true for me."

I prosper wherever I turn.

The belief I choose to accept is that I either attract or repel prosperity.

All is well in my world.

As you observe the incredible power and order of the universe, you may struggle with the idea that life is purposeful, with no accidents or victims rather than life being full of circumstances that just happen. People have become paranoid, living fear-filled lives. Scientists, doctors, police departments, politicians and the military spend billions of dollars to "protect" the vulnerable "victim", thereby enhancing the acceptance of a "victim" mentality.

This unquestioning acceptance will not change until we learn to reclaim our rightful power and take charge of our lives. Once you eliminate your fear beliefs, *you will be safe!* If you don't believe this, then the only person or thing to protect yourself from is *yourself!!*

EVERYTHING IN YOUR LIFE IS
A REFLECTION OF THE INNER YOU.

113

Life is all about choices and the major choice is whether or not you choose to live in fear, constantly on the defensive, or whether you choose to live a vibrant, fulfilling life within a safe universe.

7 TAKE HEED OF THE POSITIVE MESSAGES

Now that you are getting close to the end of this book, I hope you have made great progress in identifying your erroneous beliefs and transforming your consciousness. Remember there are no rules, "supposed tos", "shoulds or should nots" in *BELIEFOLOGY*. There is only recognition, awareness and the knowledge that beliefs, emotions, intent and expectations form your day-to-day life and you are always free to respond to experiences, people and events in whatever manner you choose. You have the power to choose your thoughts and direction. But always remember that responsibility and ownership of your feelings and beliefs *does not imply guilt*! If you do attract sickness, accidents or victimhood there is no need to feel guilty. Or when you see others attract negative experiences to them, there is no need to be judgmental. As you become more aware of your beliefs, you will attract less unfavorable or negative events and people.

After reading *BELIEFOLOGY* you may begin to notice the "negativity" around you. Just turn on the television or read a newspaper and you will see the mass-hysteria caused by people playing the "blame/shame game" -- those people who are attempting to find the reasons for the violence and the decline of moral values by placing the blame on *someone* or *something*. They demand "more justice", or they want to see more remorse from the accused. Or they want harsher punishments and stricter laws. Then there is the rampant fear and paranoia caused by "authorities" with their alarming studies that seem to always start out with "Beware of the dangers in . . . ." Let me remind you that all the health food, security systems, rigid laws, better schools or more prisons will not protect or keep you safe if your consciousness is full of fear and punishment beliefs.

In the coming years, while the old paradigms and institutions crumble, the masses will debate, argue and attempt to cling to the very thing that causes the problems -- judgment, the belief in reward and punishment and victimhood. Just as a thunder storm clears the air, mass collective consciousness will draw in those national dramas such as the "O.J. trial", the "McVeigh trial", and sensational stories about adultery and political indiscretions. Through these real-life soap operas, the grass roots public will eventually come to terms with the realization that the common theme/cause in each one is fear, judgment, doubt and the belief that humans are by nature bad, weak, vulnerable and need to be protected and controlled for the good of both the individual and society at large. But the irony is that often it's the same theme of fear and judgment that drive both the accused and the accusers! Eventually the public will see the hypocrisy of capital punishment and *finally* understand that violence -- on either side -- begets violence.

≈ ≋ ≈ ≋

Reclaiming your inherent natural power in order to be inner-directed in consciously forming a life of choice is a process. You may find yourself getting hooked into judgmental, negative gossip with friends or work associates. These types of conversations can be extremely contagious. Try to change the conversation or just walk away. It's always your choice and there are no rules. Once you eliminate more and more judgment from your mental and emotional diet, the less you will draw negative people into your reality. The same applies to the negative programs and messages in the media. Try to focus on the positive, favorable programs, music or news. Obviously, I'm not suggesting that you can shield yourself from exposure to everything negative, but as you grow in consciousness you will have a natural propensity towards finding joyous, life-affirming information and entertainment.

Whenever you feel vulnerable and caught up in negativity, there are many ways to help you move into a more preferred state of being. There are hundreds of self-improvement and motivational videos and cassette tapes available. I keep a series of cassette programs in my car to listen to whenever I am driving.

Take time to listen to songs that will inspire and empower you with their positive messages, especially songs that refer to the interconnection between humans and nature. There are so many songs with uplifting, joyful, optimistic powerful lyrics. Remember the song about high hopes and that persistent ant?

Watch movies that express the power of human strength and unconditional love. Remember what the good witch told Dorothy -- she had the power to return home all along. The power was within her!!

While you are on your journey to becoming more inner-directed, you will be subjected to many influences that will affect your thinking. Why not choose inspirational media that raises your dreams no matter what your race, sex, age, health status or income level? Once I changed my beliefs, the most difficult part of *BELIEFOLOGY* for me was trusting my inner-self to attract only the most favorable situations in all areas of my life. Media and friends who reinforced unconditional faith were a big help. If you can just "get out of your own way", you will find life is mystical, magical and full of blessings!!

8 UNCONDITIONAL LOVE

The universe expresses love through every fiber of your being, just as it's strength energizes the earth through the sun, wind and rain. It exudes. But there is great strength in gentleness, and the universe also delicately caresses each member of creaturehood while it creates beautiful flowers, dewdrops, fragile natural designs, trees, exotic plants and other wonders of nature. This universe and all of its creations are propelled into existence by the most powerful energy of all: _UNCONDITIONAL LOVE_. The major intent of ALL THAT IS, as well as the motivating force, is _ETERNAL LOVE_.

You have heard the expression, "There is nothing more constant than change." Well no relationship, whether it be intimate, simply friendly or a business liaison, ever remains the same but is forever evolving and growing, sometimes in different directions. Unconditional love has no conditions or limits on how you love, how you express love, whom you "should" love or who should love you. Our society has created a framework of bondage requiring proofs and guarantees of further love through establishing institutions of marriage, based on documents of promises creating laws and conditional expectations. When those expectations aren't met, threats lead to disharmony and culminate in divorce. Then instead of two consenting adults dissolving their marriage, it requires an outside authority (divorce court) with all of _its_ legal ramifications.

When you reclaim your inherent rightful power and make your own commitments without relying on outside authorities such as a marriage license or clergy, then if an end is necessary, you will also be able to negotiate your own separation.

It's both ironic and sad that we rigidly control love and the intense feelings it produces. You cannot destroy _real_ unconditional love, for like energy you may manipulate it's flow but you can't destroy it. How can something as free as love be censored or controlled into requirements, contingencies and systematic systems of dogma? To love and to be loved unconditionally allows you to accept yourself and others unconditionally. There is no judgment with true love.

It's beneficial to extend this same freedom to your emotions. Our culture has a precedence of suppressing, repressing and depressing emotions instead of consciously analyzing emotions to find their mental causes or the profound spiritual understanding and insights that they can lead to. You wouldn't be human if you didn't have emotions, any more than you could have the earth without weather. Try not to separate and divide your emotions into good and bad or right and wrong. Rather you should trust your feelings (even those that are aggressive, hateful or negative) and allow them to flow. You will discover that even negative emotions are temporary and often lead to love and peacefulness. Like a thunderstorm precedes a new, beautiful, fresh sun shiny day, anger and frustration can lead to calm, happiness and elation if you are open to it. Be at peace with yourself and affirm your own rightness and accept all parts of yourself, including the negative, and you will find that eventually you will activate more of your positive aspects. While you're loving and accepting yourself unconditionally, you will automatically extend this unconditional love and acceptance to others who will in turn honor themselves and enhance the conscious, collective awareness of the eternal connection to ALL THAT IS (or God or whatever you want to call it).

We usually attach hate with bad. But although it is a temporary separation from love, hate is often filled with a desire to be accepted and a need to return to love itself. If you examine people in painful relationships, full of hate, you will often find that there is caring or their feelings wouldn't be intense enough to hate. A further exploration of this hate may reveal fear, judgment, guilt or basic powerlessness. Unconditional love doesn't mean you must accept an unhappy relationship and stay stuck in it. Unconditional love means the right to choose and that choice could mean two individuals going their separate ways while simultaneously accepting their unique differences. This real love allows a dearly loved one the freedom to leave no matter how painful the departure may be. Be open to the fact that there is a "good-bye" to every relationship (platonic, family, intimate or business).

Emotion is the fuel that projects ideas and desires into motion. Love is the emotional energy that makes the world go around. ALL THAT IS (God) loves itself into a being that replicates herself/himself/itself into physical manifestation. You are an extension, an expression of that essence. Fulfillment, harmony, ecstasy and happiness are the emotions of the soul-self that bring to the outer world freedom, spontaneity and productive creativity and beauty. Give of yourself, even if it is just a friendly smile, touch or gesture, to a stranger or a lonely soul.

LIFE AND LOVE IS WHAT YOU PUT INTO IT.

One of my favorite references to love just happens to be my favorite verse in the Bible. Although I feel the Bible is misinterpreted and I don't believe it's the "ultimate truth," nevertheless the following passage is an excellent description of love:

1 Corinthians 13:

If I speak in the tongues of men and angels, but have not love, I am a noisy gong or a clanging cymbal,[2] and if I have prophetic powers, and understand all mysteries and all knowledge, and if I have all faith, so as to remove mountains, but have not love, I am nothing.[3] If I deliver my body to be burned, but have not love, I gain nothing.

4. *Love is patient and kind; love is not jealous or boastful*
5. *it is not arrogant or rude. Love does not insist on its own way, it is not irritable or resentful;*
6. *it does not rejoice at wrong, but rejoices in the* right;

Love bears all things, endures all things.

8. *Love never ends; as for prophecies, they will pass away; as for tongues, they will cease; as for knowledge, it will pass away.*
9. *For our knowledge is imperfect;*
10. *but when the perfect comes, the imperfect will pass away.*
11. *When I was a child, I spoke like a child, I thought like a child, I reasoned like a child; when I became a man, I gave up childish ways.*
12. *For now we see in a mirror dimly, but then face to face. Now I know in part, then I shall understand fully, even as I have been fully understood.*
13. *So faith, hope, love abide, these three, but the greatest of these is love.*

During the summer of 1967, we witnessed the "summer of love". A generation that talked about "flower power" and "do your own thing." Freedom and the "love" word became common. However, with all the debates on freedom, we were far from free because of past conditioning and erroneous collective beliefs. Nevertheless, this period of time was the advent of the revolution of mass consciousness. This dawning found people questioning authority and going through a process of unlearning erroneous beliefs. The older generation at the time, especially conservatives, thought it was appalling and anti-patriotic to question the federal government, especially on such issues as the Vietnam War. Now it's in vogue for even the older generation and conservatives, young and old, to distrust the federal government and question it's motives and polices.

Conditional love is based on powerlessness, fear and not trusting self. The prerequisite to living and loving unconditionally is unlearning limiting beliefs.

The '60's brought us women's liberation and the equal rights movements; the '70's and '80's saw gays coming out of the closet. In the '90's, men began introducing themselves to their feminine aspects while women were integrating their male aspects. More and more we see the "coming out of the closet" of all human beings as we realize and accept all of our multi-dimensional selves, including our spiritual oversouls as well as our intuitive natures. Instead of identifying with any one race, culture or religion, when asked we will proudly answer, "I am part of the human race."

Gradually few will deny the effects of the changing paradigms as the old paternalistic, hierarchical institutions tumble and are replaced with real democratic (people's power), cooperating, empowering and more equitable systems. Social services will replace the concept of "client" with the new concept of empowering the consumer, and will privatize much life-managed care, truly becoming consumer/customer driven.

Also, the close relationship and connection humans have with the alive, breathing mother earth will become more apparent. Like the human species, the earth is in labor, delivering the universe a new earth/human consciousness. This transformation will bring growing pains resulting in erratic weather conditions, earth changes and adjustment changes for each and every individual as she or he evolves personally. Have patience and trust in your own abilities and the world at large to respond constructively through this metamorphosis and continue to remind yourself, your loved ones and your neighbors that this revolution is temporary. When unconditional love, human compassion, social conditions, economic prosperity and unconditional acceptance of self and others catches up with modern, sophisticated technology, then men and women will work and live from a point of power and will assume 100% responsibility for their co-creations.

Now is the time to reclaim your power. *Be still and know that we are all Gods and Goddesses, co-creating a future of unconditional love, unlimited abundance, universal peace and eternal happiness.*

ๆ ๆ ๆ ๆ

Our future selves will look back at us and be amused that we spent so much time, energy and money on creating complex and complicated systems, theories and formulas based on things outside of ourselves, always requiring outside proof or validation in the form of formal, "official" quantitative evidence. Individually – and collectively – we will eventually discover that we were chasing our tails. The answers to our questions and our self-fulfillment were within us all the time. Religion and science will merge into true spirituality where religion will focus less on eternal life and more internal life, and science will explore inner-space instead of outer space.

I have spent my whole life in search of the reasons and purpose of existence. Now I realize the purpose of life is to have fun with life: creating and fulfilling ourselves; following our inner guidance; and enjoying this wonder-FILLED physical and spiritual adventure.

Now it's time to ask yourself:
What do *you* believe?
What do *you* know?

ABOUT THE AUTHOR
ও ৯ ও ৯

Ken Routson is a management consultant, author, visionary, educator and entrepreneur. He has served as Chief Executive Officer for several corporations, including a healthcare agency. Ken is nationally recognized for his contributions in the field of disabilities. Because of learning disabilities, he had difficulty with language until he was in the sixth grade. Ironically he now makes his living speaking.

In 1984 he formed *Individual Growth and Fulfillment*, a consulting company that assists individuals and agencies to be empowered, enabling them to proactively create their future. He travels across the country conducting seminars and workshops on stress reduction, self-improvement and empowerment, as well as motivational and prosperity classes. Ken also offers private life coaching sessions.

Ken incorporates the principles of BELIEFOLOGY in everything he does. This book, *BELIEFOLOGY: RAISE YOUR CONSCIOUSNESS TO WEALTH, HEALTH AND HAPPINESS*, is a culmination of his many experiences.

Other materials by Ken Routson:

BELIEFOLOGY: RAISE YOUR CONSCIOUSNESS TO WEALTH, HEALTH AND HAPPINESS is now available in a 4-disc CD set.

BELIEFOLOGY WORKBOOK -- Filled with exercises that will help you put Ken's Beliefology theories into practice in your daily life.

INTERNAL LIFE: I DO BELIEVE IN SPIRIT -- Follow along as Ken examines his life journey and learn to use your life's magical coincidences to create a reality of abundance, joy and health.

We hope you enjoyed this Tulip Press publication.

To order additional copies of *BELIEFOLOGY*:

Call: 513-942-3009 ◆ Shop **on-line at:** www.beliefology.com.

Or for shop-by-mail convenience:
Send a check or money order for $14.95 + $5.00 s/h to:
Tulip Press
POB 181212
Fairfield, OH 45018

BELIEFOLOGY makes a wonderful gift to give to family and friends. Just let us know whom the book is for and we will make sure it is personalized and autographed by Ken Routson.

List name of recipient(s):

_____

_____

Other titles by Ken Routson
available from Tulip Press:

◆ *Now available on CD:*
BELIEFOLOGY:
RAISE YOUR CONSCIOUSNESS TO WEALTH,
HEALTH AND HAPPINESS

◆ *BELIEFOLOGY WORKBOOK*

◆ *INTERNAL LIFE: I DO BELIEVE IN SPIRIT*

Look for our latest title available soon...

Excerpted from:

TRUST AND ALLOW
THE PROCESS OF LIFE IN-JOY!
by Leslie Stewart

"... sometimes in your existence in your day to day activities someone may approach you and they are not necessarily stroking your ego-self in a positive manner but in a manner that seems disheartening to you or makes you feel less than what you were prior to the meeting. When you become more self-directed and self-empowered, you will no longer have those needs for outer validation whether it be from co-workers, bosses or systems.

For when you are indeed trusting the Universe and allowing yourself the freedom to know that all is well in your world regardless of any outer circumstance, you are indeed being the whole self, and the divine connection to All That Is will not be severed – only if you allow it to be so. So congratulate yourself, love yourself, be at peace with yourself, and know that when you indeed trust and allow the process of life to flow through you, you are proving to yourself and no one else that you are indeed connected."

᭕ ᭚ ᭕ ᭚

Leslie Stewart has been studying and living metaphysics for over thirty years. She has worked in the medical field and studied *Body Talk*, a mind-body method that recognizes the body's innate ability to heal itself on all levels. Ms. Stewart conducts seminars around the country and offers individual consultations in person or by phone or e-mail. For more information contact Tulip Press at 513-942-3009.